Money

Guide to a Secure Retirement

by the Editors of Money Magazine

Edited by Junius Ellis

CONTENTS

CHAPTER ONE

The New Realities of Retirement

IN CONTRAST to previous generations of Americans, people in the third quarter of life today are more likely to view retirement as a time of renewal and adventure than a restful reward for a long career. Indeed, the evidence is overwhelming that we are now in the golden age of retirement. Social Security benefits have never been higher. The number of company pensions and savings plans has multiplied over the past decade. Innovations such as Individual Retirement Accounts and Keoghs were unknown to retirees of earlier generations. Not only do prospective pensioners stand a better chance of living better than they ever could, but they also are freer to choose when to call it a career. Although the standard retirement age remains 65, both early retirement and late retirement are catching on.

Contributing to an early departure from work are attractive financial packages that growing numbers of companies offer to older employees. Working longer is on the upswing for quite different reasons. Since 1978, federal law has prohibited companies from making retirement mandatory for anyone except top-level executives. Career switching and part-time work late in life are more acceptable—and available—than before. Experts attribute the expanding job pool for older people to the national shift from a manufacturing economy to a service economy. The result is greater opportunities to start a new career in your sixties and to capitalize on your lifetime of experience and skills.

What's more, the generation nearing or in retirement is the wealthiest in United States history. These people bought houses cheap after World War II, prospered during the postwar economic boom, saw the value of their homes inflate during the 1970s and paid far less into pension plans and Social Security than they will take out. Much of their wealth is in real estate; nearly three-fourths of people over 65 own their own homes. Half of the couples retiring have a pension from a public or private employer. That can give you remarkable freedom to decide just how much you want to work, and when, and where. You can yield to passions and causes that you may have put off for years, from travel adventures to a whole new world of post-graduate study.

The goal behind both the acquisition of family wealth and saving for retirement is financial independence—and the opportunity to make the most of it. Alas, the price of this unprecedented opportunity is the increasingly complex planning required to build, protect and pass on your bundle to the next generation. And success is based on a premise that used to be unthinkable: Americans want to provide for their families and then retire with no reduction in their standard of living.

The purpose of this book is to help you achieve that lofty goal, regardless of your age. We will not beguile you with the notion that it is easily attained. To the contrary, you face many vexing issues and tough decisions. How much will you need and how much can you reasonably expect to have to finance life after work? Can you really count on Social Security? How much protection does your company pension offer? Where should you invest your IRA, Keogh and company-sponsored savings plans? You will find answers to these and other key questions in this guide. But keep in mind that retirement planning is no longer a concern of only those persons within a few years of calling it a career. Every stage of your life—from your thirties to your forties and fifties—requires different strategies and a keen appreciation of trends that will directly affect the elderly and their families.

For example, a baby recently born in America will turn 65 in a geriatric society in which one in every five persons is that age or older. This will be the inexorable result of major demographic changes that are unfolding all around us. The age seesaw of our population, once weighted by the young, will tilt heavily toward the old because the baby boomers are maturing and the average life span is increasing. Life expectancy at birth could reach 80 by the year 2000, compared with 70 in 1965.

This trend means that extended families will no longer be primarily horizontal, comprising brothers and sisters and cousins. Instead, they will turn vertical: three and four generations of a single family will be alive at once. Already the average married couple has more living parents than children. It means that spouses will spend more years together after their children have left home than they did raising them. It means that the average woman will spend more years caring for her aging mother than she will have spent caring for a child.

Even more significantly, it means that a whole new set of hazards line the twisting path to a secure retirement. Most notably, families now stand a greater chance than ever before of having a disabled elderly relative to support. Those who do not prepare accordingly risk undermining the financial planning of two or even three generations. Given increased longevity, more and more parents are likely to have children who themselves are over 65. A quarter of the aged need some type of long-term care—and the age group that most often does, those over 85, is the fastest growing.

In the past, almost all of them would have been taken care of by families, frequently by a daughter in her mid-fifties. But the ability of families to care for the elderly is weakening now that some 60% of women 45 to 54 are working. Indeed, the most reliable predictor of a disabled older person's chances of entering a nursing home is the absence of living children or their presence in the labor force.

Profiling Today's Pre-Retirees

HOW STURDY is your present nest egg? If you are in the most intense retirement planning years—between ages 45 and 64—see whether the following profile sounds anything like you:

- You are a superior saver, putting away 14% of your annual income versus 4% for Americans overall, and look forward to a full life after work.

- You don't plan to move to a less costly house after retirement, yet you don't expect your standard of living to drop in step with your income.

- You haven't done much planning, which could be dangerous. For instance, your biggest worry is inflation, but one of your main investments is a savings account, the least inflation-resistant of all.

These attributes are shared by most of the 600 pre-retirees interviewed in a study commissioned by Merrill Lynch and released to MONEY. The most encouraging finding: nearly one in five of those surveyed said that they save 20% or more of their income, a figure that rises with age. According to the study, pre-retirees' greatest fears center around having enough money to carry them through retirement. Inflation tops the list, indicating an understanding of its insidious effects on the purchasing power of fixed-income pensions and annuities. If inflation were to rise, say, two percentage points, your income would be cut in half in 10 years. Fret as they may, however, about half of pre-retirees prefer to stash their retirement money in inflation-eroding savings accounts. Only about a quarter buy stocks, historically the best inflation hedge, and half said they have little or no confidence in the stock market.

The great majority of pre-retirees see long-term health care as an important issue. Yet nearly two-thirds of those surveyed are untroubled about their ability to pay for long-term care. The only plausible explanation for such optimism is that respondents believe employers and the government should be responsible for three-quarters of long-term health-care costs. While long-term care is often on the congressional agenda, employers are unlikely to expand benefits.

Similarly, most pre-retirees think that the responsibility for providing their retirement income should be divided equally among themselves, their employers and the federal government. And most believe that they will collect the Social Security benefits to which they are entitled. But the younger ones, the 45- to 49-year-olds, are least sanguine on the subject of Social Security. Only half of them feel that they can count on Social Security versus three-quarters of the 60- to 64-year-olds. Whatever your views, don't assume that what you collect from the government and your pension will equal your savings contributions. Many experts say that you will be lucky indeed if Social Security and your pension provide half of your retirement income.

On average, the pre-retirees surveyed estimated that they will need roughly 70% of their current income to live comfortably during their retirement years. The figure is generally in line with guidelines that retirement planners often recommend. To live as well as you do now, however, you probably will need at least 80% of your current income.

While work-related costs will decline in retirement, younger retirees in their fifties and sixties are likely to increase sharply their discretionary spending on travel and other leisure activities. Out-of-pocket medical costs will also escalate as you grow older. And you can't count on the equity in your house to bail you out. The house-price inflation of the mid-1980s gave homeowners a windfall beyond the home equity they would normally have built up during their working lives. Over the next 20 years, housing prices on average are likely to rise by only about one percentage point more a year than the rate of inflation for the period.

Whenever you finally decide to retire, you are bound to encounter some sleepless nights. You have to worry about whether there will be enough money to live on until the end of your life and your spouse's. If you are to get a pension lump sum, you must suffer the anxieties that you might invest it poorly and live out the latter years of your life as a burden to your children. Even if you invest wisely, you will have to contend with the nightmare of all retirees: no matter how smart and provident you are, inflation hurts you in the end. If you move too hastily to some putative paradise, you might wind up repenting your mistake at excruciating leisure. And you must wonder how you'll escape the paralyzing boredom that afflicts so many who no longer have jobs.

Fortunately, the survival strategies for the future are at hand. Families that learn to talk to one another candidly about sensitive topics—Do Mom and Dad have a will? Shall we ask the children about moving?—will thrive. So will people who see retirement as a glorious mixture of work, play and learning. After all, growing old can be viewed as a kind of second adolescence. Like the first one, it is fraught with exhilaration and fear of the unknown. The important difference is that this time you are bringing wisdom with you, and the experience should be that much sweeter.

CHAPTER TWO

The Dream of Financial Independence

DOES ANYBODY remember leisure time? Not long ago, this delightful free period ran from about 5 p.m. to 11 p.m. Monday through Friday and then made a return appearance lasting all weekend long. It was the time to read, garden, muse, to do what you wanted to do. Today, leisure time is a scarce commodity. One Roper poll found that half the population feels pressed for time and noted that participation in hobbies has plunged. For example, only 37% of people now call music one of their hobbies, compared with 47% a decade ago.

Are frazzled workers destined to fizzle? Not a chance. Many are just knocking themselves out now so they can afford to retire early and make leisure their next full-time activity. The numbers speak for themselves: as the average life expectancy has risen—to roughly 72 for men and 78 for women—the age at which people retire has tumbled. Today the average retirement age is around 61; in 1970 it was 65. Millions of Americans these days are declaring their independence—in their fifties, forties and even thirties. For them, retirement has come to mean almost anything except shuffling off to play shuffleboard. Today's youthful retirees often run part-time businesses, volunteer at social service agencies, take their hobbies seriously and travel the globe.

You have probably thought about how you would spend the time you earned after retiring early. Whatever your dream, the chances of attaining it are far better than you might imagine. Financial lures abound for people who cut loose while still young. A survey of 763 large employers by the Wyatt Co., a benefits consulting firm, shows that 93% paid pensions to retirees at age 55 or earlier if they had served at least a specified number of years, usually 10 or 15. More Americans are eligible to receive pensions as a result of federal legislation that requires companies to cut vesting time from 10 years to either five or seven. Company-sponsored savings programs, IRAs and Keogh plans offer tax-advantaged ways to build cash for an early retirement. And Social Security benefits may not be substantially reduced if you stop working before 62, the age when you can start getting the government checks.

Early retirement is not for everyone, of course. Some can't afford it. In a MONEY survey, having enough money for retirement was the No. 1 financial worry for people 35 to 49. You might not be able to get out early if you are facing tuition bills for your children's education well into your fifties. Your pension may be inadequate (or nonexistent) if you hopped jobs or work for a small firm. Others are psychologically unprepared for early retirement. You may not be ready either to give up the camaraderie of business associates or to spend a lot more time with your mate. Sometimes, one spouse wants to retire early but the other doesn't. More often, this scenario involves a woman who wants to stay on because she entered or re-entered the work force late or only recently landed a really challenging job. Fear of boredom is genuine for those who can't figure out how they would occupy days without deadlines.

For those intrigued by the concept of early retirement, the main prerequisites are preparation, creativity and dedication. You will have to reposition your investments while working to amass the pot needed at the early-retirement age you select. Quitting early obviously means that your savings must last longer than otherwise. Assuming a 4% average annual return after inflation, someone planning to retire at 55 has to sock away $560,000 to collect $30,000 a year until age 90, compared with $468,000 for someone waiting until he is 65. The younger retiree also has 10 fewer years to accumulate that 20% additional cash reserve. Shrewd investing alone will not swing early retirement for everyone; there may well be some necessary trade-offs to weigh in the future. You may have to make sacrifices either before or after you retire, like cutting back on luxuries or entertainment expenses.

The more creative you are earlier, the less spartan you will have to be later. Try to devise ways of building your own retirement annuity, not through an insurance company but through your own skills. Ask yourself: what could I do now that will bring in steady annual income after I retire? The answer might be honing a hobby that you will turn into a sideline business in retirement. It might be buying rental real estate today with a mortgage you will have paid off by the time you retire, thus practically guaranteeing a tidy, positive cash flow. Or it might be picking up a new skill by taking night classes (see "Working after Retirement" later in this chapter).

The expertise you gain could eventually become rewarding in all respects. But consulting, the most popular form of post-retirement entrepreneurism, ideally requires building contacts and a reputation before stepping down from your current job. Trying to market yourself as a consultant after you quit working can end up taking more time than you spent at your old job. If your dream of independence involves running your own business, you had better get started now. Many service companies operate during nights and weekends and require no more start-up capital than the cost of a personal computer, laser printer, fax and telephone-answering machine. Among them: advertising copywriting, travel-agency ticketing and tutoring.

Even if you are not contemplating a second career, you should start gearing up today to make sure you have enough money to carry you through retirement. First, estimate how much annual income you will need after stopping work. You will have to replace only about 70% to 80% of your current earnings, because you will no longer rack up costs of employment such as commuting and a business wardrobe. Many Americans move into less expensive housing or cut expenses to reduce their burden or to hasten their retirement. But don't forget to factor in inflation between now and your target date—a calculation that might require help from an accountant or a financial planner. Then find out what annual income you can count on from pensions and Social Security. Your employee-benefits department can help with the former; call the local office of the Social Security Administration for the latter. Remember, your company pension probably won't be increased annually with inflation as Social Security checks are. The total will leave you with an annual shortfall that your investments, including any contributions to company savings plans, will help fill. Next, add in money you expect to get from any personal annuity you create.

Most early retirees make their break thanks to corporate pensions. Though many large companies reduce pensions by as much as 50% if you quit work at 55, about half let employees leave at 62 without any cut in their pensions. It generally pays, however, to keep working until you reach the age when your employer removes or sharply scales back its early-retirement penalty. Say you are 55, have worked at the company for 30 years and earn $50,000. Assume your company calculates your annual pension benefit as 1% of your final salary times the years you worked there. But it will pay half that amount if you quit before 60. Retire now and your annual pension will be $7,500. But if you wait until 60, when yearly raises of 5% would boost your salary to $63,800, your yearly pension will be $22,300, or about three times as much.

Even though your pension check will almost always increase the longer you work, leaving your job before 65 may not cost as much as you think. Some experts argue that working past 60 can actually cut the total value of your future benefits in current dollars. Pension formulas typically increase your annual benefit more slowly after age 60. As a result, the only financial benefit you might receive from working an extra year would be that year's salary. Ask your company benefits counselor what your pension will be if you leave at various ages, both on an annual basis and as a lump sum. Then have your accountant or financial planner figure out when your pension will stop growing enough to make working longer worthwhile.

In recent years, many companies have offered special early-retirement packages that sweeten pensions for employees who volunteer to accept these offers. Some early-retirement deals are worth grabbing, but others are strikingly stingy. (For guidance on how to evaluate such arrangements, see Chapter 5: "Taking Charge of Your Company Retirement Plans.") Note, however, that an often overlooked pension penalty, introduced into tax law in the 1980s, may have the effect of discouraging some high earners from retiring early. Anyone retiring at 55 cannot collect more than a maximum annual pension benefit (the amount varies with your salary scale). This

Are You Really Ready To Retire?

WHILE YOU may be all set for a financially secure retirement, you may not realize how much life after work can draw on your emotional reserves. If you suddenly find yourself with 40 or more hours a week of free time that you haven't adequately prepared for, you could be headed for trouble. These questions, based on the findings of gerontologists and psychologists, will help you determine how well prepared you are for the day when the alarm clock no longer rules. Answer each question that applies to you. Then tally the points assigned to each answer for your score. At the end, see what the specialists think.

	YES	NO
• Will you be able to cut back your hours at work gradually instead of all at once? *Change may exact a toll if it's too abrupt. Making the transition slowly gives you time to adjust at your own pace.*	+3	-3
• Are you married? *Being unmarried can reduce an individual's life expectancy more than smoking or being overweight.*	+4	-4
• If you're married, is the relationship satisfying? *Retirement can put a strain on your marriage. If you don't get along before you retire, chances are things will get worse afterward.*	+2	-2
• If your spouse is working, will he or she retire at about the same time as you? *An increasingly common problem occurs when the husband retires while his younger wife continues to work; it often reduces his self-esteem and creates confusion about household duties.*	+3	-3
• If you're not married, do you live with someone? *Although being in a satisfying marriage is the best way to overcome feelings of isolation, living with someone is a close second.*	+3	-3
• If you live alone, do you have daily contact with family or friends? *This is another substitute for a live-in companion.*	+2	-2
• Do you have at least one person outside of the office—for example, your spouse, a friend, even your banker or broker—in whom you can confide? *Even if you rarely share intimacies, just the presence of a confidant is essential.*	+4	-4

	YES	NO
• Do you have a place at home or outside of it where you can have total privacy? *Together is fine up to a point. Everybody needs a retreat.*	**+2**	**-2**
• Do you try not to hang around the office after the workday is over? *If you're spending too many hours at work, you may be dependent on the job for social life. Letting go will be hard for you.*	**+3**	**-3**
• Have you made any new friends outside of work this year? *Don't make the mistake of assuming your work colleagues will still have time for you after you retire.*	**+3**	**-3**
• Are you involved with community, church or cultural groups? *Such activities may prove to be the center of your post-work days. Don't wait until retirement to get involved outside your job.*	**+4**	**-4**
• Do you schedule activities—fishing trips, museum visits, picnics—to fill up your free time? *Retirement may well be the first time in 40 years that you will control your own time. You should know how to plan your days without a boss looking over your shoulder.*	**+3**	**-3**
• Have you taken part in an intellectual pursuit, such as attending a class or lecture, or a physical one, such as a competitive sport, in the past month? *Aim for a variety of activities. Just because you like fishing doesn't mean that after retirement you will enjoy it every day.*	**+2**	**-2**
• Have you learned something new—say, a foreign language or gourmet cooking—in the past five years? *Taking on new challenges shows an openness to change.*	**+2**	**-2**
• Were you able to adjust easily when your children left home or during other periods of major change? *If you have been able to weather most of life's changes, you'll almost surely adjust well to retirement.*	**+4**	**-4**
• Are you looking forward to retirement? *Your attitude can cast a shadow over everything. A negative one could become a self-fulfilling prophecy.*	**+3**	**-3**

If you score 18 points or above, you are on solid footing. Between zero and 18, you have some catching up to do. Below zero, you need to work hard on improving your emotional preparation for retiring.

ceiling rises for people who retire at age 62 and again for those taking pensions starting at 65. Consult with your accountant; many companies may be able to skirt these ceilings by paying any higher obligations out of company reserves, rather than pensions.

Social Security is also less Scroogelike to early retirees than you might expect. True, your checks at 62 could be 20% smaller than if you waited to start receiving them at 65. But a closer look at the numbers shows that the government actually promotes early retirement when computing Social Security benefits. Consider, for example, a 55-year-old male middle manager with a typical earnings history. If he retires now, in seven years he will begin getting a Social Security benefit of $843 a month, in today's dollars. If he keeps working until 62, his monthly benefit will be $901, only 7% more. Thus, if this man works seven more years, his extra payoff from Social Security will be peanuts.

The outlook for early retirement in the future is partly cloudy. Since a company plan will typically freeze your pension amount from the time you leave until its regular retirement date, inflation will melt a portion of your benefits. The aging of the U.S. population will also bring with it some ominous thunder for younger members of the work force. The ratio of employees to retirees at many major corporations has slipped from about 15 to 1 in the 1970s to around 4 to 1 lately. That means as the baby-boom generation nears retirement at the turn of the century, companies will need to hang on to more employees. Early-retirement packages may be curtailed lest businesses end up paying retirees almost as much as employees.

Congress has approved scheduled changes that will snip Social Security benefits for early retirees in the next century (see "Social Security Simplified," Chapter 4). But by then, nearly a generation of Americans will have struggled throughout their youth for the delicious opportunity to tell their boss to take the job and shove it. Their reward will be an enticing opportunity to spend a full, idyllic third of their lives in well-plotted leisure. And the pleasure of leisure is something no government check can match.

Working After Retirement

CHANCES ARE there's another job in your retirement, even if you won't need the pay. What with longer, healthier lives and earlier, richer retirements, Americans face a prospect that would have startled their parents and left their grandparents incredulous: decades of active, useful living after they receive the golden handshake. What sensible person whose life has largely been defined by work would want to laze through so many potentially fruitful years? Here are no-nonsense answers to some of the first questions you are apt to ask yourself about that next big step.

Why should I work after I retire? To begin with, you may have no choice. Inflation, poor planning and an inadequate pension may force the issue. And even if you don't need a job to make ends meet, you may decide you want one just to keep active and healthy—benefits that become more crucial as you get older.

Does it pay to keep working? If you're well off, you could wind up losing money by working. Social Security and tax code provisions penalize people who earn too much in retirement. For example, if you go back to work between the ages of 62 and 64, you will lose one dollar of Social Security benefits for every two dollars you earn above certain income limits. Between 65 and 69, you give up one dollar of benefits for every three dollars earned over specified limits. Once you reach age 70, you can earn as much as you like without penalty. In addition, you are taxed on up to 50% of your Social Security benefits if the total of your adjusted gross income, non-taxable interest, and half your Social Security benefits exceeds $25,000 ($32,000 if you are married). If that total exceeds $34,000 ($44,000 for couples), you owe tax on up to 85% of your benefits. If you keep working past 65, your benefits will rise by a certain percentage each year until age 70. These increases range from 3% to 8% depending on the year of your birth.

How do I decide what type of job is right for me? Like most retirees, you may want to stay with what you know, but on a part-time basis. If you have the zest for a change, do some homework at a library. Ask for *The Occupational Outlook Handbook* or *The Encyclopedia of Careers and Vocational Guidance.* Both provide detailed information on hundreds of careers. Some of the most successful second careers spring from a lifelong dream, a hobby or an interest shared with a friend. Also talk with people who are working in occupations you think you might enjoy. Once you've made your choice, you can launch a job search.

When and how should I begin planning my retirement career? Start as soon as you can—certainly well before you call it quits at your present job. If you want to change fields, begin planning at least five years before you retire. This will give you time to take classes and meet people in your field of interest. Even if you want to stay in the same field, it's a good idea to research potential employers a year before your planned retirement.

What's the best way to find a job? Most career counselors answer this question with a buzz word: networking. Make a list of everyone you know—friends, relatives, business relations, old school chums, even distant acquaintances—who may be able to help you find a job, whether it is in your old field or a new one. You can often make useful contacts at career seminars or by joining professional organizations. If you don't know anyone at a company you are interested in, try to find out the name of the person who has the power to hire you. Look in the *Reference Book of Corporate Managements* or *Standard & Poor's Register*, available at most libraries. Or phone the personnel department at the company. Then write a letter to that executive detailing your skills and interests. After a week or so, follow up with a phone call. Be cordial but persistent. Typically, you will have to be interviewed by 20 to 30 people, and it may take anywhere from three months to a year before a job offer materializes.

Will I be offered a lower salary because I am receiving a pension? The practice still exists at many companies, but habits are changing. Federal law protects older job seekers from arbitrary hiring and salary discrimination. And employers are coming to appreciate that older workers are usually well worth full pay. If you are asked your salary expectations, be assertive. To protect yourself from being shortchanged, find out what the average salary is for the position you want. Career counselors or library research can help. Should you meet the job qualifications for a position in your old field, it's only fair that you should request the middle to high end of the salary range. If you are changing fields and need additional training, you should expect your salary to be at the low end of the scale.

Should I prepare for conflicts with younger colleagues? The best preparation is the confidence of knowing that you're probably more experienced and more reliable than younger workers. If you feel someone is treating you unfairly because of your age, discuss the matter in a friendly, professional manner. If your troubles continue, you can complain to your superior. If you are at least 40 years old and the person causing your difficulties is in a higher position, you can complain to your local Equal Employment Opportunity Commission office. The commission will investigate to determine whether your accusation has merit. If the EEOC probers find your grievance valid, they typically will try to resolve it by conciliation before taking an employer or individual to court. You can also sue independently, but that can take months.

Should I consider starting my own business? Probably not. While independence sounds exhilarating, don't forget that 66% of small businesses fail within five years, often because of poor planning or lack of funds. Before you embark on what could be a financially and emotionally devastating experience, ask yourself the following questions (more than one or two nays should give you pause): Do I have a product or service that's really needed? Do I have financial backing or money of my own that I can afford to lose? Am I happy working alone? Most telling, do I consider myself a risk taker? Someone who's been a middle manager at the same company for

30 years may not have what it takes to become an entrepreneur. If you are convinced that you are one, seek advice from people who have started their own businesses. The Service Corps of Retired Executives, sponsored by the Small Business Administration, provides free advice on starting your own business. Look for SCORE's address in your telephone directory under U.S. Government/SBA/SCORE.

Where can I go for job training and placement? Your first and best source is your present employer. More and more companies offer job planning and counseling. Another option is to call your state job training or employment service (look in the telephone book under State Government Offices). Many have listings for older workers or can at least direct you to placement services in your area. Private career counselors provide occupational testing, one-on-one counseling and training in job-search skills. But if your employer doesn't pay the fees for you, be prepared for charges that can run into the thousands. Another excellent source of help is the growing number of nonprofit organizations set up to assist older workers. The American Association of Retired Persons sponsors AARP Works, an employment planning program available in more than 100 locations. For information, write to AARP Works, AARP Fulfillment, 601 E Street, N.W., Washington, D.C. 20049. You can also write for nonpaying consulting work to the National Executive Service Corps (257 Park Avenue South, New York, N.Y. 10010), a volunteer placement service for retired executives. Small and medium-size businesses often recruit through its Senior Career Planning & Placement Service.

How can I try out a new career? If you don't need to work for money, by all means explore the field of volunteering. Often this can later turn into a paid job. Among the advantages of starting this way: You can set your own schedule and contribute your time to a cause that may give you great satisfaction. Volunteer opportunities abound in hospitals, day-care centers, schools and other community organizations.

CHAPTER THREE

How to Reach Your Goals

HAVING MONEY in the family. What an idle dream it seemed when you started out in your first apartment with a few wedding presents and a batch of furniture the Salvation Army would not take. Your rent seemed bigger than the national debt and, to make ends meet, you drove an Own-a-Wreck and survived on a diet of meatless meat loaf.

Now that you have progressed in life and career, it's easy to see how your standard of living has advanced. If you are in your forties or fifties, you may be surprised to discover when you tot up your assets that you have accumulated a stunning sum. If you are younger, you may be amazed at your potential for doing so. Wealth—a term once reserved for the few—is beginning to touch the many. An estimated 1,500 families are worth at least $100 million, and several thousands more around $50 million. Internal Revenue Service surveys of estates reveal that 850,000 people had assets of at least $500,000, and half a million owned more than $250,000.

Most people on their way to such wealth consider themselves solidly middle-income folks who will work, save and invest their way to upper assetdom. Yet with affluence comes responsibility. On the one hand, there is the risk of mismanagement and loss; on the other, the opportunity to enlarge your net worth, to secure your retirement nest egg and to pass some of it along to your heirs. This chapter lays out the basic game plan for evaluating and reaching these goals. Subsequent chapters will discuss in detail how to tailor strategies to your family's profile. Developing a plan that works best for you demands time, discipline and the guidance of specialists, such as financial planners, experienced in negotiating the maze of wealth management. But that's a small price to pay for the luxury of knowing you and your children will be provided for.

Start your asset-building program by making the most of what you have. You should pay close attention to your employee-benefits plans, particularly those to which you contribute. They have gained greatly in value because they allow you to stack up tax-deferred savings. Examine your investments: there may be sensible ways to invest that you have never thought of. Your house is probably the foundation of your family wealth because its value has boomed over the past decade or so. Yet it may diminish in relative importance in the future even though its appreciation keeps pace with inflation. By coordinating these three elements, you can achieve both security and growth:

Your benefits. The funds stored in your employee-benefits plans may well turn out to be the stars of your future personal finances. That is because these plans typically offer more opportunity for tax-free buildup and more choice of investments than you might otherwise have access to. While every company has its own wrinkles, employee-benefits plans fall into two major categories: defined benefit and defined contribution.

The first, which has been around for decades, is simply your pension plan. Defined benefit means that the company puts away money for you and decides what you get—based on a formula—when you retire. Spurred by tax breaks for themselves as well as their employees, more and more companies have added defined-contribution plans. These allow employees to put aside a portion of their salaries in a fund to which the company also adds. There are two types of such plans: matching programs, in which a company contributes a specified percentage—usually 50%—of what you invest, and profit-sharing arrangements under which your employer adds a portion of profits to your savings. Additionally, you may be offered an employee stock-ownership program (ESOP). Your employer will typically match up to 50% of the amount you invest in shares of company stock.

In both types of plans, defined benefit and defined contribution, funds accrete quietly and inexorably until they total surprisingly large sums. At one company, a $55,000-a-year design engineer who left after 21 years of service walked away with $314,000 from various plans. An ESOP would have added even more. The National Center for Employee Ownership found that employees who earned $35,000 a year at companies with ESOPs can generally leave their jobs after 20 years with proceeds from an ESOP of more than $200,000.

Defined-contribution plans offer far more opportunity for wealth building than do pension plans. If you leave your company, you can take all your contributions with you, and the company's contribution vests more quickly than in pension plans (usually after one to three years of employment). Furthermore, many companies let you contribute to these plans as part of 401(k) salary-reduction programs. That's the best deal of all because it puts you three giant steps forward. First, you can stoke a 401(k) with up to roughly $9,000 pretax—the exact amount increases annually with inflation—although most employers impose lower limits. Second, you get an immediate gain on your investment because your employer usually matches a portion of your contribution. Finally, the earnings are not taxed until you begin withdrawing them at age 59.5. If you change jobs, you can roll over the funds into an IRA that continues the tax-deferred buildup.

Perhaps even more important, defined-contribution plans usually give you more than one investment option. The choices may include your company's stock, diversified portfolios of stocks and bonds that operate much like mutual funds and guaranteed investment contracts—loans to large insurance companies that promise a fixed rate of return slightly higher than bank certificates of deposit. With most plans you can choose between two different types of investments, usually a growth fund and an income fund. If you are close to retirement and are leery of taking risks with your money, you will probably want to choose an income fund or guaranteed investment contract that pays steady dividends. If you have just started your career, however, you may prefer to invest for growth in stock funds. Although you may invest when the stock market is about to take a dive, such moves are partly offset by the company's matching contribution. The same holds true for your ESOP. Even if your employer's stock sags, the match will compensate for temporary drops in value.

When you retire, your company may offer you several payment options for your pension. The two most common choices are a monthly check or a lump sum, which is typically based on your length of service, final five years' pay and life expectancy. Deciding which option to take requires detailed computations. The wealth-building point that many Americans are learning to take with increasing seriousness: if you believe you can invest the lump sum profitably enough to equal the pension you would otherwise get, you can also leave behind a sizable legacy. An added incentive: the tax bite on lump sums taken at retirement can be moderate. Almost everybody who retires after age 59.5 is eligible for five-year forward averaging, which lets you spread out the lump as though it were paid in equal installments over five years. While the entire tax bill must be paid the year you receive the lump sum, forward averaging will significantly lower your bracket.

Your investments. One factor you should take into account in designing your investment portfolio is the security of your income. That is because people's investment inclinations often mirror the way they earn their money. For example, a freelance writer, a musician or a salesperson on commission might earn $35,000 one year, $60,000 the next and $10,000 the third year. Yet these are the types of people who tend to invest in chancy emerging growth stocks, risky venture-capital deals and highly leveraged real estate projects. Such an individual might instead be better off hedging with safer vehicles—CDs, Treasury bills or mutual funds with holdings in stocks that pay dividends and promise some growth. By contrast, a corporate employee with a secure job who earns $50,000 a year and has a generous, diversified portfolio in his employee-benefits plans is often inclined to invest his spare cash in a safe but stodgy mutual fund. In this case, the person can obviously afford to look for a little more bang in his personal investments.

If your analysis of your income tells you that you should be investing some of your spare cash more aggressively, but you are the type of person who frets over every decision, you might adopt a strategy called dollar-cost averaging. With this technique, you merely pick a mutual fund that matches your investment goals and tolerance of risk and invest equal sums periodically. This way, you will be purchasing fewer of the fund's shares when securities prices are high and more when prices dip. To make dollar-cost averaging work, you have to have the discipline to keep writing those regular checks even when your investment plunges. No-load growth mutual funds are ideal vehicles for this approach.

Another wealth-building avenue is to invest in mutual funds inside tax-deferring envelopes such as rollover IRAs. (If you are covered by a company pension plan and earn more than $25,000—$40,000 for a couple—you can no longer fully deduct your contribution to a standard IRA.) Single-premium deferred annuities, sold by insurance companies, operate in a similar fashion. You buy an annuity with after-tax dollars, but your gains accumulate tax-free. Some annuities promise a specified annual return; others may offer a choice among as many as 15 different funds and allow you to add small deposits monthly or quarterly so that you can dollar-cost average. You have to choose carefully, however, because many insurance companies extract hefty fees.

Your house. This remains the most valuable asset most families acquire. The Census Bureau has estimated that a house represents about 41% of a typical family's worth. Housing economists, however, are not forecasting the same heady gains for houses that they enjoyed in the inflation-ridden late 1970s and early 1980s. Expect instead that single-family houses will track inflation over time. That means your home will more likely be a source of capital preservation than capital growth.

Owning an asset whose value keeps pace with inflation is just one of the reasons for pursuing the American Dream of home ownership. For example, making regular payments on the mortgage is a method of disciplined savings that works well for those who would normally spend every dollar they earn. Owning a house also qualifies you for one of the few remaining tax shelters available to individuals: deductions for property taxes and mortgage interest. When you sell, you can defer taxes on the profits if you put them into a new house within two years. And at age 55, you can exclude $125,000 of your gain from taxation.

However impressive the fortune you ultimately create, you probably will have a harder time in the future ensuring that your family—and not the IRS or your state—is your prime beneficiary. Currently, estate taxes do not inhibit the passage of wealth within most families; the federal tax code exempts assets totaling $600,000 for individuals ($1.2 million for a husband and wife). Above those limits, the IRS takes 40% to 55%. So if you and your spouse die at the same time and leave $1,200,001, the most the estate will owe in federal taxes is 40% of $1, or 40 cents.

Those generous limits are being scrutinized by an increasingly stingy Congress, which is threatening to toughen death taxes. Raising the percentage that the IRS can claim, scaling back the exemption for individuals and couples and taxing appreciated assets are all ways that Congress may choose to respond to the pressure to increase revenues and help reduce the budget deficit.

No matter how confiscatory estate taxes become, it is still better to have created a small family fortune than not. And who knows what it might grow to in another generation or two.

Figuring What You Will Need

OF ALL the major milestones in life—graduating from college, say, or getting married—leaving work may be the only one where the decisive consideration is whether you can afford to do it. Indeed, financial independence does not come cheap. It means being able to support your pre-retirement standard of living for as long as three decades in the face of an unpredictable economy and implacable inflation. Financial security in retirement isn't a birthright; to get it you have to plan for it.

The first step in setting your goals is to decide how much income you will require in retirement. If you are more than 10 years away from calling it quits, you obviously won't be able to predict your retirement expenses accurately. But the worksheet on page 30 will help you form a reliable estimate. Then, you can compare this amount with figures on another worksheet, on page 34, used by financial planners to determine how much you

The Actual Costs Of Your Retirement

WHILE NEARLY everyone looks forward to retirement as a time of doing as one pleases, there are as many ways to pursue your pleasures as there are people. That's an important retirement planning point, because the stuff of your post-working-life dreams—be it Caribbean cruises, relocating to the sunbelt or simply working on your golf score—helps determine how much money you should be putting toward those goals now. The rule of thumb among financial planners and benefit consultants is that you will need an annual retirement income amounting to 70% to 80% of your current earnings.

Whatever the life style you envision, the best way to ensure that you can pay for it is to plan as far ahead as possible. The first step is to determine what your annual expenses are likely to be. The worksheet on the facing page is specifically designed to help you do that. Despite the diversity in retirement living, financial planners surveyed by MONEY note at least some similarities in spending patterns after age 65. For example, most retirees spend about the same amount on food, gifts, charitable contributions and personal care as they did while working. Medical and dental bills, on the other hand, are significantly higher, depending on how generous your company's retirement coverage is. Here are some general guidelines to help you fill out the worksheet.

Line 1: If you pay off your mortgage and take care of all necessary maintenance problems before you retire, housing costs should drop by as much as 25% to 30%. Count on even more shrinkage if you sell your house and buy a smaller one. Condominium owners and renters should factor in maintenance-fee and rent increases. And anyone who plans to spend more time at home should anticipate higher utilities charges.

Line 2: Financial planners estimate that if you are moving from business suits to jeans, you can expect to reduce clothing expenses by 20% to 35%.

Line 4: Scratch commuting costs. Other transportation expenses will increase if you intend to be very active. Planners recommend that two-car couples keep both autos during retirement, especially if both are fairly active.

Line 6: Most people keep giving the same amounts to charitable, political and educational institutions, as well as to family members outside the immediate household. But the overall figure drops, usually by the amount you used to give at the office.

Line 7: If your kids will be grown by the time you retire, you can eliminate education expenses, unless you plan to help pay your grandchildren's college bills. And if you intend to return to school yourself, check into reduced tuition costs for senior citizens.

Line 8: There will be little change in your payout for property, liability and auto insurance, but retirees can generally reduce their life insurance coverage by at least 50% or, if their spouses are fully provided for under their pension plan, eliminate it altogether.

Line 9: If you are currently covered by a company health plan, expect medical and dental costs to spurt by about 50% because of increased illnesses combined with reduced insurance coverage. Medicare pays only part of doctors' fees and hospital bills. Check your company's coverage for retirees.

Line 10: You should plan to be debt-free by the time you retire, thereby eliminating loan repayment expenses.

Line 12: How much you spend for entertainment depends on how active you are. Expect such expenditures to rise an average of about 20% during your retirement.

Line 13: Budget for higher veterinary bills if you will have an aging dog, cat or other pet.

Line 14: While your contributions to pension plans cease at retirement, many financial planners encourage clients to continue setting aside about 10% of their income as a hedge against inflation.

Line 15: If you don't work, it's farewell to Social Security (FICA) taxes. Also, check laws in your state because some don't tax income from retirement plans. You will be taxed on up to 50% of your Social Security benefits if the total of your adjusted gross income, nontaxable interest, and half your Social Security benefits exceeds $25,000 ($32,000 if you are married). If that total is over $34,000 ($44,000 for couples), you'll owe tax on up to 85% of benefits.

Line 16: With more adult kids expecting financial help from Mom and Dad and Americans' increasing longevity, you could be contributing to the down payment on a child's first house while paying for a parent's nursing home.

Total current expenditures should equal 100% of your current before-tax income. By dividing your total expenditures at retirement by your current gross income, you will arrive at the percentage of your current income that you will need in retirement.

Expenditures	At retirement	Current year
1 Housing. Rent, mortgage, property taxes, utilities (gas, oil, electricity and water), telephone, home furnishings, household services, maintenance, improvements	______	______
2 Clothing. Purchases and cleaning	______	______
3 Food. (including tobacco and alcohol)	______	______
4 Transportation. Car repair and maintenance, installment payments, gas, commuting costs, other	______	______
5 Gifts.	______	______
6 Contributions.	______	______
7 Education.	______	______
8 Insurance. Life, medical, auto, property, liability	______	______
9 Medical and Dental Care. Premiums, deductible and out-of-pocket costs	______	______
10 Loan-Repayment Costs.	______	______
11 Personal Care. Grooming, health club, other	______	______
12 Entertainment. Vacations, dining out, movies, plays, concerts, sports events, cable TV, videocassettes, entertaining, sports, hobbies, other	______	______
13 Pet Expenses.	______	______
14 Savings and Retirement. Contribution to company plans, IRAs, Keoghs, SEPs, other savings, investments	______	______
15 Taxes. Federal, FICA, state, local	______	______
16 Support of Relatives.	______	______
Total Expenditures. (add lines 1 through 16)	______	______
Total Current Expenditures Divided By Current Gross Income.	______	
Total Expenditures At Retirement Divided By Current Gross Income.	______	

will need to maintain your standard of living later on. By measuring your income needs against the resources you will have in retirement, such as Social Security and your company pension, you can calculate how much capital you must accumulate. Equally important, you can use this information to implement a savings plan.

As you get closer to retirement and can estimate your budget more accurately, you are likely to find that you can get by on less. By the time you are ready to call it quits, for example, you may well have paid off your home mortgage and the bills for your children's education. With your kids finally grown and presumably self-sufficient, you may feel free to reduce your life insurance. And if you move to a warmer climate, you can expect to save on heating bills. On the other hand, be sure to allow for larger discretionary expenditures such as travel and education. Be prepared also to spend about 30% more on medicine and health insurance.

The unpleasant surprise of retirement planning is that the combination of Social Security and pension benefits is unlikely to give you the income you need. Even if you spend a couple of decades with a fairly generous employer, you can generally expect the combination to replace no more than 40% to 60% of your salary in the first year you are retired. The rest will have to come from the capital you build up in your IRA, your Keogh plan, your personal investment portfolio and any tax deferred savings offered by your employer, such as a profit-sharing or 401(k) account.

How much capital will it take to make up that gap? A married couple retiring at age 65 should figure on about $179,000 of capital for each $10,000 that their pension and Social Security benefits fall short of their yearly income needs. Thus, if you need to replace $25,000 of annual income in retirement, the price of a worry-free retirement would be nearly $450,000.

Part of the reason you require so much capital is that the money has to last as long as you do. The median life expectancy is 20 years for a man at age 60 and 25 years for a woman. Thus, you have a 50% chance of outliving the life expectancy assigned to you when you retire. As a result, it's wise to base your planning on the assumption that you will live longer than 85% of the people your age. For example, a 60-year-old man could feel secure with savings sufficient to meet his income needs to age 90; a woman of the same age should lay in enough to reach 94.

The other contingency that boosts the cost of financial independence is inflation. Because your Social Security benefits increase in step with the consumer price index, your benefits will continue to provide the same proportion of your retirement income in later years as in the year you left work. Few private employers' pensions are indexed to inflation, however. Consequently, your capital must be large enough so that it earns more than you need to live on, leaving you a surplus to reinvest. Later, as inflation pushes your expenses ahead of your investment earnings, you will have enough stashed away to meet the added need by dipping into principal without having to worry about running out of money ahead of schedule.

While the sums you may have to save for retirement may seem imposing, the job of accumulating them needn't be—if you start early. Assuming your investments grow at the conservative pace of three or four percentage points over the inflation rate, you could build a retirement chest of $179,000 (in today's dollars) by saving only $6,600 a year for 20 years. The calculation includes the amounts your employer contributes to your tax-deferred savings plan at work, if you began 20 years before you retire. If you postpone saving until you are only 10 years from the finish line, you would have to set aside more than $15,600 a year.

Help From Planners

IF YOU'VE already set unambiguous retirement goals and are confident that your assets will add up to what you will require when you stop working, the advice you can get from a broker on investments, an attorney on estate planning and an accountant on tax matters may be sufficient. But if you're a haphazard saver or you don't relish coordinating advice from several professionals, then you should consider hiring a financial planner.

How Much Should You Save?

THE WORKSHEET at right will tell you roughly how much you need to start saving now to hold on to your standard of living in retirement. The multipliers used in lines 7, 9 and 11 allow for inflation by assuming your investments will grow at three percentage points over the inflation rate, before and after retirement. This keeps all figures in today's dollars.

Line 3: You and your spouse can ask your local Social Security office to estimate the annual benefits you each have earned, or you can calculate them yourself with the help of a Social Security fact sheet called *How Your Retirement Benefit is Figured.* (For a very rough estimate of your benefit, fill in $13,000 if you make $42,000 or more; if you make between $20,000 and $42,000, enter between $8,700 and $13,000.)

Line 4: Your company benefits department may be able to estimate your pension. Make sure the estimate assumes that you continue working until your retirement age at your current salary. Employing that method will somewhat understate your likely eventual payout at retirement but will keep the figure in today's dollars.

Line 7: The multipliers in column A incorporate the cautious assumption that men will live to 90 and women to 94—longer than 85% of them do now. Single men should use the multiplier under "men." Women and couples should use the one under "women," since wives usually outlive husbands.

Line 8: Your personal retirement portfolio includes any investments you have specifically earmarked for retirement, aside from your IRA or Keogh. For your employer-sponsored savings plans, check the most recent statement from your 401(k), profit-sharing, thrift or stock ownership plan and total your vested balance in each.

Line 12: Consult the most recent annual statement from these plans to find the amount your company contributed on your behalf to each of the plans last year. Enter the total.

AGE AT WHICH YOU EXPECT TO RETIRE	MULTIPLIER A men	MULTIPLIER A women
55	22.1	23.5
56	21.8	23.2
57	21.4	22.8
58	21.0	22.5
59	20.6	22.1
60	20.2	21.8
61	19.8	21.4
62	19.3	21.0
63	18.9	20.6
64	18.4	20.2
65	17.9	19.8
66	17.4	19.3
67	16.9	18.9

TIME UNTIL YOU EXPECT TO RETIRE	MULTIPLIER B	MULTIPLIER C
1 year	1.03	1.000
3 years	1.09	.324
5 years	1.16	.188
7 years	1.23	.131
9 years	1.30	.098
11 years	1.38	.078
13 years	1.47	.064
15 years	1.56	.054
20 years	1.81	.037

1. Current gross income ____________

2.. Annual income needed in retirement, in today's dollars
(70% of line 1) ____________

3. Annual Social Security retirement benefits ____________

4. Annual pension benefits ____________

5. Guaranteed annual retirement income
(line 3 plus line 4) ____________

6. Additional retirement income needed
(line 2 minus line 5) ____________

7. Capital required to provide additional retirement income
(line 6 times multiplier from column A at left) ____________

8. Amount you have saved already

____________	+	____________	+	____________	=	____________
personal retirement portfolio		IRA/Keogh		employer-sponsored savings plans		total savings

9. What your current investments will have grown to by the time you retire
(total from line 8 times multiplier from Column B at left) ____________

10. Additional retirement capital required
(line 7 minus line 9) ____________

11. Total annual savings still needed
(line 10 times multiplier from column C at left) ____________

12. Annual employer contributions to your company savings plans ____________

13. Amount you need to set aside each year
(line 11 minus line 12) ____________

The kind of help you'll require and how much you should pay for it depend largely on what you can realistically afford and when you hope to retire. Some planners offer tax planning, legal counsel and investment advice in addition to broad strategies for meeting your goals. Most will sell you such investments as insurance, for which they earn commissions. Fees are often steep. Full-blown initial plans, which typically cover every aspect of your financial life from here to the grave, cost from $500 to $5,000. Only wealthier clients, whose finances are complex, should have to pay the higher fees.

In searching for a financial planner who's well suited to your family, be sure to ask candidates how they are compensated and what you will pay. For example, you should be careful of those practitioners who say that their plans are free because they live on commissions earned on products bought by clients. Such planners could be tempted to sell you what you don't really need. You should lean instead toward fee-only or fee-and-commission planners, who tend to be more objective.

If you're still in your twenties or thirties, a financial planner can help you build assets to meet interim goals and give you a jump on building a retirement nest egg. Planning becomes more critical after you enter your forties. As your children scatter, your career progresses and your assets accumulate, you can begin to set retirement goals based on more realistic projections of earnings, investment returns and inflation. Along the way, a financial planner can help you set more rigid guidelines for saving toward retirement.

The closer you are to calling it quits, the fewer your financial options—and the simpler your retirement-planning needs. You may be able to find answers to your most important questions for around $1,000—the price tag for some first-rate planners who offer formal pre-retirement studies. Others will sell you a chunk of their time for typically $100 or more an hour. Write to the Institute of Certified Financial Planners, 7600 E. Eastman Avenue, Suite 301, Denver, Colorado 80231, for a list of member planners located in your area. In addition, many large companies have pre-retirement seminars for employees.

CHAPTER FOUR

Weaving a Sturdy Safety Net

ALTHOUGH IT is never too late to start saving for your retirement, the ideal time to begin the process is soon after you go to work. Like it or not, the government automatically imposes the discipline with its payroll tax for Social Security—the old-age safety net for most Americans. For all the concerns about the fiscal health of the retirement program, you can still count on Uncle Sam to pay benefits through at least the first decade of the next century. After that, Social Insecurity could possibly arise as the large baby-boom generation reaches retirement age. Likely measures to accommodate this bulge of new beneficiaries include higher payroll taxes and cutbacks in the portion of your pay replaced by your monthly government check.

What can you really count on from Social Security? This chapter provides answers as well as a detailed blueprint for enlarging your basic nest egg.

The best conduits for personal retirement savings are tax-advantaged accounts that magnify returns by allowing investment earnings to compound tax-free until withdrawal at retirement or upon disability. The old standby, the IRA, may still make sense if you are eligible to deduct the annual $2,000 contribution from your taxable earnings. Better yet are fully deductible contributions to company-sponsored savings and profit-sharing plans (discussed in the next chapter) and their Keogh cousins for self-employed workers and moonlighters. If your employer doesn't offer a tax-sheltering retirement savings vehicle, your insurance agent or stockbroker almost certainly does.

Social Security Simplified

DESPITE PERSISTENT fears that the government's retirement program will fold, Social Security is here for the long term. True, the program needed bolstering in the 1980s to ensure benefits for workers now nearing retirement. But the system will be on firm footing when today's 40- to 60-year-olds retire. Theoretically, Social Security could go bankrupt early in the next century when today's young workers retire; politically, there's little chance that such a debacle will occur. Instead, the rules will change in ways no one can now predict with absolute certainty.

So try to put aside the rhetoric and start analyzing the benefit you almost certainly will get. A 65-year-old can retire now and receive up to $13,536 a year—the amount increases annually with inflation. Generally, you must work 40 quarters or 10 years before Social Security will pay you a retirement benefit. Not everyone who works that long will get a check. If you are paid by a nonprofit organization, such as a museum or hospital, most of your working years probably won't count toward earning a Social Security benefit. Only employment since January 1, 1984 at a nonprofit institution will be used in the benefit formula, unless you've paid in Social Security taxes all along. About one-third of employees of state and local governments and most federal employees hired before January 1984 aren't covered by Social Security. Federal government workers hired since then, however, are covered.

The Social Security Administration pays full benefits to employees who retire at 65 and cuts payouts for workers who quit earlier. You can't apply for your own retirement check until age 62, and it will be 80% of the amount you would get by waiting until age 65. Starting in the year 2000 and lasting through 2022, the early-retirement benefit for a 62-year-old will be nipped by about .8% a year. So by 2022, early-retirement checks from Social Security will be only 70% of full benefits.

Social Security rewards workers who put off their benefits past 65. Soon the lure will be more enticing. Today, Social Security enlarges your retirement check by 4% for each year you delay taking full benefits between age 65 and 70; that's in addition to the annual cost-of-living increase. The delayed retirement credit inches up a bit, increasing by one-half of 1% every other year, until it reaches 8% in 2008. But it doesn't make sense for people approaching retirement to put off taking Social Security benefits at 65 just to get a larger check later. The extra money you receive from the delayed retirement credit won't equal the Social Security income you could have been accepting starting at 65.

The retirement program also sticks it to some people who just can't bear to call it quits. For example, if you are aged 62 through 64, the government cuts your Social Security benefits by one dollar for every two dollars you earn over certain limits, lately $7,680, that increase yearly with inflation. Workers aged 65 through 69 must give up one dollar of benefits for every three dollars earned above the limit, lately $10,560, again indexed for inflation. Once you reach age 70, however, you can earn as much as you like without penalty.

Social Security won't start sending you a check until you notify the local office that you're ready. File an application three months before you want the first monthly check to arrive and be sure to bring or send a certified copy of your birth certificate. If you expect a check for your spouse's benefit, you will need a certified copy of your marriage license. Divorcees filing for benefits have to present certified copies of marriage and divorce papers. In the January check, benefits automatically rise by the increase in the previous year's cost of living. If inflation is less than 3%, however, Congress must vote to raise Social Security checks by that amount.

If you're married but only one of you works, Social Security will send you one monthly check equal to 1.5 times the worker's entitlement, provided the beneficiary doesn't start collecting until age 65. A nonworking spouse who collects Social Security at 62 will get only 37.5% of the worker's benefits. A working couple with only one spouse employed long enough to receive a full Social Security benefit at 65 will also get one monthly check of 150% of that spouse's entitlement. If the lower-earning spouse didn't earn enough to get a Social Security benefit equal to more than half the high-earning spouse's, the couple will also get a single check of 150% of the bigger benefit. Couples entitled to two full benefits are mailed separate checks, unless they request a single monthly payment. A divorced single person can get the spouse's benefit at age 62, as long as the couple were married at least 10 years.

Women frequently can choose between collecting Social Security based on their own employment or taking a joint benefit based on their husbands' earnings.

Financial planners urge working women to send for a statement of their Social Security earnings record once they reach age 55. (For details on obtaining your records, see "Sizing Up Your Future Check" later in this chapter.) Then, the woman will know whether she has worked long enough to get a full benefit. If she hasn't, she might want to work a little longer to qualify. After that, she can compare her own benefit with her husband's to figure out whether they would be better off receiving one check based on his earnings or two checks based on their combined salaries.

From Social Security's inception in 1937 through 1983, all benefits were free of federal, state and local taxes. Not any more. Today you are subject to federal taxes on up to 50% of your Social Security benefits if the total of your adjusted gross income, nontaxable interest, and half your Social Security benefits exceeds $25,000 ($32,000 if you are married). What's more, if that total exceeds $34,000 ($44,000 for married couples), you owe tax on up to 85% of your benefits. Say your adjusted gross income is $25,000, and this year you will get $10,000 in Social Security benefits and $5,000 in tax-exempt interest. You add half your benefit, or $5,000, and all the interest to your income for a total of $35,000. So if you're married, you will exceed the $32,000 cutoff by $3,000, and you will add half that, or $1,500, to your taxable income. In addition, many states tax Social Security benefits. By the time baby boomers, born between 1946 and 1964, reach retirement, about half are likely to find their benefits taxed. The primary reason: the federal formula's thresholds currently aren't indexed to inflation, and in 30 years or so, many more retirees will have incomes exceeding them.

No one knows exactly how Social Security will cope with the work force's evolution from yuppies to grumpies. By 2020, nearly twice as many people are expected to be collecting Social Security checks as today. Yet at that time, there should be only 2.4 workers paying Social Security taxes for each retiree. In recent years the ratio was about 3 to l; in 1945, it was 42 to 1. This much seems clear: everyone who pays into the system will get a Social Security benefit.

Common Questions On Social Security

SMART FINANCIAL planning demands that you and your family understand how Social Security's retirement, survivor and disability systems work. But Americans have become increasingly confused about the intricacies of the programs. The following questions and answers will help you sort through the tangle of Social Security rules.

What kind of benefits can I get? The Social Security system consists of three funds that pay benefits to Americans. The Old-Age and Survivors Insurance Trust Fund provides monthly checks to retirees, their families and to families of deceased workers. The Disability Insurance Trust Fund pays benefits to disabled workers and their families. The Hospital Insurance Trust Fund pays Medicare claims.

I'm 30, expecting a baby and planning to leave my job for a few years. How will that affect my benefits? As long as you eventually accrue 40 quarters of coverage, you will still get retirement benefits. The checks may be the same size or slightly smaller than if you didn't take time off.

I'm married but have never worked for pay. Will I still get a Social Security retirement benefit? You will receive a benefit equal to 50% of your husband's or wife's by meeting three tests: you have been married at least a year, you have not earned enough Social Security coverage to get your own retirement benefit equal to more than 50% of your spouse's, and you wait until 65 to receive the benefits. If you start collecting the checks at age 62, your benefit will be only 37.5% of your spouse's, not 50%.

I was married for 15 years before I divorced my husband, and I have never worked for pay. Am I entitled to Social Security benefits as his former spouse? If you were married at least 10 years, have been divorced for at least two years and remain single, you are eligible for spousal benefits at age 62. If you remarry at 60 or later and then retire, you will get benefits based either on your current spouse's earnings or your former spouse's, whichever are more. Note, however, that if you tie the knot before 60, your first marriage won't count for Social Security purposes.

I'm 35 and have a wife and a young daughter. If I die tomorrow, what will Social Security pay them? Based on your age, your family will get special survivors benefits if you have accumulated six quarters of earnings out of the last 13—that is the equivalent of roughly 1.5 years of work. Your child under age 18 will receive 75% of your retirement benefit until she turns 18, up to a limit that increases annually with inflation. Your wife will get 75% of your benefit as long as she is caring for a child under 16; she will receive your full benefit when she is 65. Those survivor payments would be smaller if you died at an older age, in part because younger families tend to need more income. Social Security will also give your family a payment of $255 toward your funeral expenses, regardless of your age.

Sizing Up Your Future Check

IN THE past, one of the biggest aggravations of Social Security was getting an accurate estimate of the benefits you could expect after retirement. If you knew the right questions, you could write to the Social Security Administration, which months later would send back, piecemeal, the scraps of information you had specifically requested. No longer. The agency now spells out your whole basket of benefits in a document called *Personal Earnings and Benefit Estimate Statement.* To get one, you simply call a toll-free number (800-772-1213) and request a questionnaire. It asks you for a number of facts about yourself, including your name, Social Security number, date of birth, previous year's earnings, current year's estimated earnings, the age at which you plan to retire and your projected earnings from now to retirement. About four to six weeks after you send in the form, you can expect to receive this list of estimates:

- Your monthly retirement check from Social Security, in today's dollars, at your stated retirement age. To arrive at this figure, the Social Security computer assumes that your future annual earnings, net of inflation, will rise at the national average of 1% a year. The earliest you can collect your check is at age 62, if you are willing to settle for 80% of what your benefit would be if you worked to 65.

• The full benefit you could get by waiting until you are age 65 to retire. Under Social Security regulations, 65 will remain the standard retirement age until 1999. After that, the age for collecting a full benefit will start to rise at the rate of nearly one month per year. Someone born in 1939, for example, will have to wait four months after his or her 65th birthday to be eligible for a full retirement benefit. From that point on, the full-benefit retirement age keeps increasing until it gets to age 67 in 2027. There it will remain.

• The larger benefit available to people your age who continue working until they are 70.

• Your survivors' monthly benefits if you die during the current calendar year. Children of Social Security taxpayers are likely to be eligible for these benefits until they reach 18 or 19, depending as a rule on when they finish high school. A spouse who stays at home with the children can also collect survivors benefits until the youngest child is 16. By taking an outside job, however, a widow or widower will probably forfeit Social Security income.

• Your disability benefits if you will be unable to work for at least a year or if you are terminally ill. Like survivors benefits, Social Security disability benefits include income for dependent children.

• A year-by-year statement of your earnings that were subject to Social Security taxes and of the Social Security taxes that you paid. Since the Social Security Administration has been known to make an occasional error in figuring benefits, you should check the numbers you get by matching them against your own earnings records. The Social Security statement also explains briefly but clearly what it takes to become eligible for benefits. Basically, you must work 10 years to earn retirement benefits; you generally must work five out of the last 10 years to claim disability benefits.

Should You Still Fund An IRA?

AS WITH Social Security, the rules governing IRAs can be unnecessarily confusing. Congress axed the full deduction for contributions by middle- and upper-income taxpayers in 1987. In their zeal to raise revenues, lawmakers cut in half the number of people who qualify for the full deduction and burdened people who make contributions to nondeductible IRAs with a lifelong snarl of paperwork. Left intact is the remaining nondeductible IRA benefit: tax-deferred compounding of investment earnings—an advantage that could be wiped out if tax rates rise by the time you start withdrawing the money.

If you are among those who still qualify for the deduction, putting the maximum $2,000 in an IRA—plus $250 in a nonworking spouse's account—still may make sense. The value to you: an investment for your retirement as well as more cash in your pocket from tax savings ($560 if you are in the 28% bracket). Those who now qualify for the full deduction include couples filing jointly with adjusted gross incomes of less than $40,000; singles with incomes of less than $25,000; and anyone who is not covered by a pension, profit-sharing or other tax-advantaged retirement plan, including simplified employee pensions and Keoghs. Partial deductions are allowed for couples earning between $40,000 and $50,000 or singles earning between $25,000 and $35,000. Their write-off drops $10 for every $50 they earn above $40,000 if married or $25,000 if single.

Whether the twin advantages—a current write-off and tax-deferred earnings—are sufficient to make a partially deductible, or even a fully deductible, IRA worthwhile depends on how soon you may need the money. If you take it out of your IRA before age 59.5, you will have to pay a 10% penalty plus income tax on the withdrawal. (After age 70.5, however, you will be penalized if you *haven't* begun withdrawals.) When those factors are taken into account, a person taxed at the maximum rate who contributes $2,000 annually to a deductible IRA earning 8% would have to leave his money untouched for more than 11 years before he turns 59.5 to beat the return he would have earned in a taxable investment at 8%. The bottom line? Even if you can take the full deduction, an IRA is sensible only if you are sure that you won't need to tap it for at least a decade.

If your contributions are not deductible, the case against making them can be overwhelming, unless you're within 10 years of retirement. Without the write-off, the real cost of your contribution rises sharply, to an aftertax $2,560 if you put in $2,000 and are in the 28% bracket. This higher real cost lengthens the time required for tax-deferred compounding to offset taxes and penalties on early withdrawals. For example, in the early 1980s, when the top tax bracket was 50%, a taxpayer who put $2,000 each year into an IRA earning 8% would have had to leave his money untouched for 10 years before age 59.5 to equal the return he would have earned in a taxable investment yielding the same 8%. But that taxpayer now must leave his money untouched for nearly two decades to match the return from a comparable taxable investment.

Yet another disincentive is the load of record keeping that now accompanies nondeductible IRA contributions. Each year you must fill out an IRS form to keep track of your deductible and nondeductible contributions. These forms must be saved for the life of your IRA. The information on them will determine the tax on your withdrawals when you begin taking money out of your account. The nondeductible contributions will not be taxed upon withdrawal; the deductible contributions, plus all earnings in your IRAs, will be taxed at your regular income tax rate.

Furthermore, your bookkeeping headaches don't end once your withdrawals begin. Every time you take money out of your IRA, you must calculate the proportion of nondeductible to deductible contributions and earnings in all of your accounts combined. Your withdrawal must then contain this proportion of nondeductible contributions and will be taxed accordingly. Say that your combined IRAs total $20,000—$2,000 or 10% of which represents nondeductible contributions. The other $18,000, or 90%, represents deductible contributions plus earnings. If you withdraw $1,000, you will owe taxes on 90% of that amount, or $900.

Fortunately, there are many attractive alternatives to nondeductible IRA contributions. Topping the list are tax-advantaged company-sponsored savings plans such as 401(k)s, discussed in detail in the next chapter. In fact, in most respects a 401(k) is actually superior to an IRA, even the fully deductible kind. A typical 401(k) allows you to put away more than an IRA and often offers other advantages such as matching contributions by your employer—plus the ability to borrow against your account balance for many purposes.

The 59.5 Solution

As Andy Rooney might ask: Didja ever wonder why you have to wait to age 59.5 to get your IRA money without paying a penalty? Why not 60? Or 55? It's like this: in 1962, Congress created Keogh retirement accounts for the self-employed and chose the day you turn 59.5 as the time when participants could start withdrawing money from their Keogh plans penalty-free. That age originated because it was halfway between 55 (the typical corporate early-retirement age) and 65 (the age for receiving full Social Security benefits).

Well, sort of. Congress took its cue from insurers' actuarial tables, which deem that age 60 starts when you turn 59.5 because you have survived more than six months of your 60th year. The logic may be byzantine, but at least this wasn't a bureaucrat's bungle. In any case, the date has become a critical milestone for anyone planning for retirement. Here's why:

- Money taken out of an IRA or Keogh plan after age 59.5 isn't subject to a 10% early-withdrawal tax penalty.

- You must normally wait until you have reached 59.5 to withdraw cash from a 401(k) or 403(b) employer savings plan without having to pay the 10% penalty. But if you are older than 55 and are retiring, you can avoid the penalty by either rolling over the savings account into an IRA or collecting the payments as a lifetime annuity. The IRS also will not impose the 10% penalty if you are disabled or if you need the money for any medical expenses that exceed 7.5% of your adjusted gross income. The process of actually withdrawing your savings plan cash is much more complex, however, as explained in the next chapter.

• You will owe the 10% penalty before 59.5 on even some withdrawals from after-tax company savings plans. These include cash from the plan's investment earnings and company matching contributions.

• The 10% penalty also applies to any investment earnings on annuities sold by insurance companies, if you withdraw the money before 59.5. Again, disabled investors are exempted, as are those who collect their money in annual payments for life.

• If you take your lump-sum pension payout before 59.5, then you cannot take advantage of the technique known as forward averaging, a calculation that significantly reduces the income taxes due on the amounts that are not rolled over into an IRA.

Why Keoghs Make Sense

KEOGH PLANS can produce much more dramatic results than IRAs for people who are self-employed or moonlight for extra income. Investors who commit to putting a fixed annual percentage of their self-employed earnings in a Keogh can make fully tax-deductible contributions of up to 20% of their yearly net income or $30,000—whichever is smaller—even if they are already covered by an employer pension or have an IRA. As with an IRA, Keogh contributions compound tax-deferred until withdrawal, can be withdrawn without penalty at age 59.5, and must be tapped beginning at age 70.5. But unlike IRAs, your withdrawals from a Keogh at retirement or upon disability are eligible for a nifty tax-saving technique called forward averaging (for details on this complicated maneuver, see "How to Make Your Payout Less Taxing" in the next chapter).

You can open a Keogh at most banks, brokerage houses, insurance companies and mutual funds. But act by December 31 if you want to shelter any of this year's earnings. Reason: only contributions to an account that exists on that date can be deducted from current-year income. Once an account is established, however, you can take a deduction for money you put into it up to the April 15 deadline for filing your return.

Although the federal government sets no minimum opening balances, institutions establish their own—typically $250 to $1,000. Annual management fees vary widely. Make sure the institution has received or applied for a letter of determination from the IRS declaring that its Keogh plans meet federal guidelines. If the institution doesn't, the IRS could disqualify it, which means assets in the account would immediately be taxed as ordinary income. If you own a business and have employees—or expect to in the near future—setting up a Keogh is more time consuming. You'll probably need to consult a tax accountant or pension consultant.

The simplest Keoghs are defined-contribution plans, so called because the maximum annual payment is fixed. There are two varieties of defined-contribution Keoghs—money-purchase and profit-sharing plans. You can put as much as 20% of your income, to a maximum of $30,000, into a money-purchase plan each year. But before opening one, be certain you can afford it. You'll have to contribute that percentage every year unless your business shows a loss. The IRS will fine you 5% of the amount of any underfunding and notify you to make up the difference within 90 days or be assessed a penalty of 100% of the shortfall.

To avoid the risk of such penalties, you may be better off with a profit-sharing plan. You can contribute only 13% of your net self-employment income or $30,000, whichever is less, but you can pick a different percentage each year, or not contribute at all. If you want to stash more than 13% but are wary of committing to higher annual contributions, you can set up two separate plans—one of each type—as long as your combined contributions total no more than 20% of your income or $30,000. If your Keogh accounts are at different financial institutions, however, you should file with the IRS, which will determine whether the combined plans conform to Keogh rules.

You may be able to salt away even more—up to 100% of your self-employment income—with yet another type of Keogh. Called a defined-benefit plan, it lets you deduct whatever you need to achieve an annual retirement income equal to the average of your highest earnings in three consecutive years. The target income can be as much as $90,000 if you plan to start withdrawing your funds at age 62 or $75,000 if you intend to retire at age 55. Obviously, the older you are the more you'll have to put away each year to reach your income goals. Detailed actuarial computations also are required because contributions to a defined-benefit plan vary according to such factors as your age, your life expectancy and the rate at which you assume your investments will grow. Each year you must submit to the IRS a form on which an actuary certifies as correct the calculations that led to your deduction. Lawyers charge $500 to $1,500 to set up a defined-benefit plan for an individual, and an actuary's certification generally costs $300 to $1,000 yearly.

If there's a major disadvantage to Keogh plans, it's the onerous disclosure forms that account owners must file with the IRS. The most cumbersome is form 5500-C, a lengthy questionnaire steeped in bureaucratic jargon. The deadline for filing is July 31—or, if your Keogh plan is tied to your fiscal year, the last day of the seventh month following the close of your fiscal year. You can get an extension by—you guessed it—sending the IRS another form. The penalties for late filing are steep: $25 a day, up to $15,000. Fortunately, you have to file a 5500-C only in the year you start a Keogh and, in most cases, every third year after that. In each of the intervening years you file a less intimidating Form 5500-R or 5500-EZ (for plans that cover sole proprietorships or partners in a partnership). Some accountants and institutions that manage Keoghs will fill out the forms for a fee, usually $95 to $250 for each document.

If you are self-employed or moonlight but loathe the thought of wading through a Keogh's paperwork, consider setting up a simplified employee pension, or SEP. This is basically an IRA with higher deduction limits. With a SEP, you can contribute and deduct roughly 13% of your net self-employment income or $30,000, whichever is smaller.

You can open a SEP at the same places that handle IRAs—banks, brokerage houses, insurance companies and mutual funds. In fact, you can use the same application form for both types of accounts. Make sure the institution knows it's a SEP; otherwise, you might have trouble putting more than $2,000 a year in the account. You can set up and contribute to a SEP as late as April 15 and take a deduction for the previous year, just like with an IRA. As with both IRAs and Keoghs, you can begin withdrawing your SEP funds at age 59.5, and you must start withdrawals by age 70.5. But if you decide to take your SEP money in a lump sum, you can't take advantage of forward-averaging to reduce your taxes, as you can with a Keogh.

Shifting Your Tax-Deferred Accounts

EVERY SPRING, banks, brokerages and mutual funds face off with one another over shares of the flood of money pouring into tax-deferred retirement accounts before the mid-April deadline for annual contributions. Even if you swore off putting new money into IRAs after tax reform, this hype fest is still a good time to assess the investments in your tax-deferred accounts and see what reallocation may be in order. Is it time to ease some cash into stocks, for example, or to lock in current interest rates on Treasury notes and corporate bonds? If so, make your move. But mind the following rules, which apply equally to IRAs, SEPs or Keoghs.

The process is quite simple if you are planning to convey tax-deferred money from one fund to another within a mutual fund family, or from one investment to another within a brokerage account. In that case, simply call your fund or broker. Just make sure that the superior (or safer) returns you project on your new investment compensate you for any sales charges and commissions you may incur. The process is more complex if you want to shift some or all of an account from one custodian to another. First you have to decide whether to have the two custodians carry out the move—a process that's known as a transfer—or to withdraw the money yourself and redeposit it in a new account. This maneuver, by the way, is called a rollover.

By transferring rather than rolling over, you avoid most of the tax-related pitfalls of moving tax-deferred money. For example, the law allows you to transfer assets as often as you wish, while it restricts rollovers to one per account within a 12-month period. In addition, when you withdraw money in a rollover, you must redeposit it in a new tax-deferred account within 60 days; otherwise the money turns into a pumpkin on which you will owe income taxes and, if you are under age 59.5, a 10% early-withdrawal penalty. In a transfer, by contrast, your tax deferral is never in jeopardy, since you never take possession of the funds.

On the other hand, you can execute a rollover in a matter of days, while transfers between custodians can take up to four weeks. Until the process is completed, the money remains invested in the original account, gaining (or losing) ground accordingly. Thus a rollover may make sense if you are trying to catch a move in the stock market or if you are switching money out of a certificate of deposit. Most banks allow you to withdraw assets from a CD without penalty only during a seven-day window following the certificate's maturity. After that, the bank simply plows the funds into another CD. So unless you initiate a transfer two to four weeks before your CD is scheduled to mature, a rollover may be the only way of extracting your retirement money before it's reinvested.

The mechanics of transfers and rollovers are quite simple. To request a transfer, ask the bank, brokerage or fund company to which you plan to relocate your money for an application form and a letter of acceptance. This paperwork establishes a tax-deferred account with the new custodian, and that company then sends your current custodian your signed letter of acceptance, directing that the specified amount be sent to your new account. To avoid delays, check with the institution holding your current account to find out whether you face other requirements before the money can be sent. For example, most companies charge a fee for closing a discretionary tax-deferred account—that is, one in which you can switch among different investments. These fees are not tax deductible, and it is better to pay them out of pocket rather than from your account balance so that the fee does not deplete the earning power of your savings.

To carry out a rollover, notify the custodian of your account that you wish to withdraw all or part of your money. You can do this either in person or by letter. (If you write, you will need to have your signature guaranteed by a bank or broker.) The company will issue you a check within five days, and you then have 60 days from the date you receive it to open a new tax-deferred account wherever you choose. You can also split the old account into several different new ones. But if you open more than one Keogh, you will have to file separate IRS forms for each plan. It is simpler to establish your Keogh at one mutual fund family or brokerage firm where you can take advantage of a variety of investments in one plan.

A Buyer's Guide To Annuities

FIXED ANNUITIES seem to possess all of the attributes that risk-averse investors crave: a competitive fixed rate of return; a guarantee that your investment will not be zapped by plunging stock or bond prices; and a shelter in which every dollar of your earnings compounds free of taxes until you make withdrawals, typically at retirement. Alas, misleading hype and the collapse of some insurers have turned these annuities into much riskier investments.

Fixed annuities are essentially simple investments that have been gussied up by the sales pitches of insurance agencies, banks and brokerages. Here's how they work: you hand over a lump sum—usually $5,000 or more—to a salesman who passes it along to the insurer issuing the annuity contract. The insurer pays a specific fixed interest rate, usually for a year, though some companies lock in rates for as long as 10 years. (Returns on variable annuities, by contrast, fluctuate with stock and bond prices.) When the rate on a fixed annuity comes up for renewal, you can reinvest at the rate then offered by the company, switch to another insurer or take your money out.

As with an IRA, interest grows tax-free until you withdraw your money. At that point, you can pull all your money out, withdraw a little at a time or annuitize—that is, turn the account's value into a monthly income stream that can run for the rest of your life. Upon withdrawal, you owe federal income tax on the accumulated earnings—plus a 10% tax penalty if you're younger than 59.5.

There are no front-end fees on annuities; the salesman's 4% to 7% commission is factored into the annuity's interest rate. But most annuities charge sizable fees for substantial withdrawals. The surrender charges are as high as 15% of your accumulated earnings for a withdrawal made in the first year of the contract and drop by about one percentage point each year until they disappear, typically in seven to 10 years. Many insurers, however, let you withdraw 10% of your account's value each year without penalty.

The best candidates for fixed annuities are conservative investors who are at least 50 years old and are willing to lock up their money for 10 or more years before drawing on it for retirement. But many fee-hungry salesmen are peddling fixed annuities to younger people who would be better off in investments offering potential long-term capital growth. For example, a recent survey of annuity buyers by the Life Insurance Marketing and Research Association shows that 37% of fixed annuities are bought by people under 50. If a fixed annuity appeals to you as a retirement savings vehicle, you can expect to sift through a lot of marketing mendacity to find the right one. There are two main types of hype today: exaggerations of fixed annuities' safety and of their investment returns.

Safety claims. Although salesmen like to point out that an annuity's value is "guaranteed," that promise is only as strong as the insurer making it. An annuity is backed by the insurer's investment portfolio, which may contain junk bonds and troubled real estate investments. If your insurer has financial problems, you may become just another creditor hoping to be paid back. For example, when the New Jersey insurance department took over bankrupt Mutual Benefit Life, the state temporarily froze the accounts of annuity holders, preventing them from withdrawing money unless they could prove a significant financial hardship.

To woo conservative savers who prefer the rock-solid security of bank accounts, banks and insurers have begun touting so-called CD annuities and certificates of annuity. The most popular of these beguiling innovations offer a one-year term, usually paying a half to a percentage point more than a comparable bank CD, with no surrender charges if you withdraw at the end of the term.

But don't be fooled by the name game. No annuities, even those sold in bank lobbies, are covered by federal deposit insurance, commonly known as FDIC. Bear in mind too that unlike a bank CD, if you withdraw money from a CD annuity before age 59.5, you'll pay the 10% tax penalty. This pinch can pretty much wipe out the yield advantage over genuine bank CDs. And even though one-year CD annuity yields beat bank CDs, they often lag yields of conventional annuities by a half to a full percentage point or more.

There's no way to be absolutely certain an insurer won't founder, but you can tilt the odds in your favor by staying with companies that get high safety ratings from at least two companies that monitor insurers' financial health. Experts suggest sticking to insurers that get an A+ rating from A.M. Best and at least an AA from Standard & Poor's, Moody's or Duff & Phelps. Your insurance agent should be able to provide you with an annuity issuer's ratings.

Rate-of-return claims. Some annuity marketers inflate their yields by playing games with the way they calculate them; others advertise sumptuous rates that have more strings attached than a marionette. The most widespread form of rate deception is the bonus annuity, in which insurers tack on as much as eight percentage points to their current interest rate. But many of these alluring bonuses can be illusory. For example, the sales brochure for one such annuity touted a "guaranteed" first-year 8% bonus on top of its 7.25% rate. But you'll get the bonus on your accrued earnings only if you eventually annuitize and take the money in monthly installments over a period of at least 10 years. If you ask for your cash in a lump sum, the insurer will retroactively subtract the 8% bonus, plus the interest that compounded on the bonus—and you'll be charged a 15% penalty on your original investment.

Even more insidious are tiered-rate annuities—so named because they have two levels of interest rates. They ballyhoo an above-average interest rate. But, as with their bonus-rate cousins, the accrued earnings in your account will reflect this so-called accumulation rate only when you annuitize your investment over a long period of time. A straight withdrawal, by contrast, will knock you down to a "surrender value" rate as low as 6% for every year you've invested.

Other insurers simply resort to the time-dishonored practice of luring customers with lofty initial rates that are lowered at renewal time. But gravitating toward annuities paying blimpish rates can be a big mistake; such annuities are frequently lousy performers over the long haul. An A.M. Best survey of the renewal rates paid each year to annuity holders by 69 insurers shows that you are generally better off opting for a competitive rate, but not necessarily the highest. Several years ago, for example, Federal Kemper Life touted a 12.25% first-year rate on its annuities, while Aetna Life & Annuity was paying a more realistic 10.5%. Three years later, however, Federal Kemper had dropped its rate to 8%, while Aetna was paying 9%. Result: after five years, $10,000 invested with Federal Kemper was worth $14,621, net of surrender charges. That was $496 less than the $15,117 value of Aetna's annuity.

To avoid being sucked in by a loss-leader rate, you

should always compare the annuity's initial rate to that of its competitors. The quarterly magazine *Annuity & Life Insurance Shopper* ($24 an issue; 800-872-6684) publishes current rates of more than 150 fixed and variable annuity policies. Then ask the annuity salesman for the insurer's renewal rates over the past three to five years. It's okay if renewal rates have gone down over those periods, provided that they've moved in tandem with some proxy of what insurers hold in their portfolio, such as the yield on five-year corporate bonds.

Many insurers say they'll protect you against low renewal rates with what's known as a bailout provision. A bailout lets you out of an annuity without surrender charges if the renewal rate slips by, say, one percentage point or more below your initial rate. You're better off without the bailout, though. For one thing, it's rather expensive. Annuities with bailouts typically pay initial rates a half to a percentage point below those without teaser rates and escape clauses. What's more, a bailout really protects you only against a company ripping you off through arbitrarily lowering its rates. If interest rates drop overall and you bail out, you probably won't be able to reinvest your money in another annuity at a higher rate anyway.

Overstating the value of tax deferral is another way some marketers make their returns look impressively high. In its promotional material for customers, Citibank has boasted that its Nationwide Life fixed annuity offers "an easy way to make 7% worth 11%," implying that a 7% return on its tax-deferred annuity is comparable to an 11% pretax return on a fully taxable investment. The brochure shows how someone in a 39% combined federal and state income tax bracket investing $25,000 would wind up with $49,178 in an annuity, versus $37,978 in a taxable investment. But that return is tax deferred, not tax-free; you eventually have to pay taxes when you withdraw those earnings. If you withdrew the money and paid taxes, the $49,178 would drop to $39,749, giving you a 4.8% annual return. If you owed the 10% tax penalty, your sum would dwindle to $37,332, or $646 less than the taxable investment, and a 4.1% annual return.

Your Life As A Tax Shelter

ONCE UPON a time there was plain old whole life insurance on which you paid a fixed premium every year to provide for your family in the event of your untimely death. While you were still kicking, the policy offered a savings account, called the cash value, that grew tax deferred at a slow but certain rate. In a financial pinch you could take your cash value and give up the policy. Or you could borrow from it at low interest and never repay the loan (the balance due would be subtracted from the policy's death benefit). If you did not cash in your insurance, your beneficiary would get the policy's proceeds free of federal income taxes when you died.

Protection and savings in the same package—could anything be simpler or more comforting? But times changed, as did the ways your cash value was invested by insurers. In particular, tax reform made life insurance that doubles as an investment one of the most enticing shelters for your retirement stash. Yet many insurance shoppers remain wary, wondering whether they should instead buy low-cost term insurance, which provides a death benefit but no savings or investment account, and do their investing on their own. Do cash-value policies really deliver? The answer, according to many financial experts, is a cautious yes.

One reason is that term gets more expensive as you age. With cash-value policies, however, your premium dollars buy far less insurance than they do with a term policy. So if you need $250,000 of coverage but cannot afford a cash-value policy that large (typical cost for universal life: around $1,750 a year for a 50-year-old male nonsmoker), buy term (around $425 in the first year, rising to $1,120 in the fifth year). Term is also the answer if your insurance need is temporary—say, you want coverage for 10 years until your children are educated.

One of the most popular forms of cash-value policies is universal life, which is essentially a combination of term insurance and a savings account that the insurer usually invests in fixed-income assets. Another possibility is variable life, which lets the policyholder choose among a broad range of investments, from zero-coupon Treasury bonds to stock and bond funds. A third choice is variable universal, a hybrid that combines the investment options of variable life with the flexible premium and death benefit of universal life.

Yet another option is single-premium life, which requires a buyer to pay the entire premium, from $5,000 on up, at the outset. Note, however, that Congress has axed single-premium's biggest attraction—tax-free loans against a policyholder's investment account—on policies bought after June 20, 1988. Now tax-free borrowing is permitted only from cash-value policies that require you to pay premiums over at least seven years.

Here are more detailed descriptions of the main varieties of cash-value policies:

Universal life. Policyholders can change both the premiums and the face amount of the policy from year to year. With universal life, money is deducted periodically from your investment account to pay for the company's administrative expenses and the cost of insurance on your life. As a result, this choice suits couples with fluctuating incomes or those who are not certain how much insurance coverage they will need.

Variable and variable universal. These policies make sense for people with reasonable risk tolerance and long time horizons. Generally, these policies offer all the conveniences of a large mutual fund family, including telephone switching among funds for free or at nominal cost. Thus policyholders can assume as much or as little investment risk as they desire, allocate their money among different kinds of funds and turn aggressive or defensive as market conditions change.

Single premium. This option is recommended for people who need some insurance and want to park a lot of cash in a safe place. Single premium comes in as many forms as there are cash-value policies; the only difference is you pay all your premiums up front. Elimination of the tax-free borrowing benefit has caused these policies to resemble single-premium annuities, which pay out periodic income for a number of years or for life but provide no death benefit. Single-premium insurance is the better buy if you plan to hold the contract until death; single-premium annuities are better suited to a retirement fund. Reason: to pay for the protection, the insurance policies typically offer returns that are one to 1.5 percentage points lower than those of the annuities.

Before deciding which cash-value insurance policy suits you best, be clear about two points. First, do not commit funds that you will need to use any time soon. Companies charge stiff surrender fees to discourage buyers from cashing in policies early. Anyone holding a cash-value policy for less than 10 years can expect to get an uncompetitive return. Second, determining whether a contract has inexpensive insurance and good investment returns is a tough assignment.

Diligent consumers can make use of two cost indexes in evaluating policies of the same type—for example, comparing one universal policy with another. Many states require companies to calculate these indexes for you. The interest-adjusted payment index is a measure of the average premium for $1,000 worth of coverage. The lower the number, the cheaper the policy. The interest-adjusted, surrender-cost index measures the current cost of cash-value policies if you were to cancel them in 10 or 20 years and take your money. This tells you your actual cost if you have to get out. Index amounts will vary with the size of a policy and the age of the policyholder, however, so a policy that represents good value for you may be a poor choice for your older sibling.

What To Ask An Insurance Agent

FEW FINANCIAL products are more confounding to the uninitiated than are cash-value policies, which give you both life insurance protection and an investment account. The following series of questions and answers can help you find the best deal.

How can I make sense of the agent's sales pitch? Your agent probably will hand you a razzle-dazzle sales tool known as the illustration—columns of numbers that purport to clarify the potential and guaranteed earnings of the policy, given your age and health. Experts often suggest that you initially ignore the illustration.

Instead, get the agent to explain the product without reference to the numbers on the page. This will test the agent's understanding of the policy and enable you to analyze fundamentals, undistracted by the salesman's pie-in-the-sky projections.

Then look at the illustration very carefully. In particular, one column of an illustration's projection of cash-value earnings assumes that current rates will continue through the life of the policy. Don't believe it for a minute. Current rates, in fact, may drop after just one month and change monthly thereafter. Another column shows the worst case for future earnings, based on the insurer's guaranteed minimum rate of return. For a more realistic view of future earnings, ask the agent for a projection based on a rate of return between the guaranteed and current rates.

What fees do I pay for a policy? Start-up fees on cash-value life insurance, including the agent's commission, can be as much as 125% of the first year's premium. Rather than take the entire bite at the outset, insurers nibble away at your account for as long as 15 years. For instance, a company keeps a certain percentage, typically 1.5%, of the earnings on your investment account. The insurer also charges you slightly more for the policy's insurance coverage than the protection actually costs. In addition, insurers might charge 2% to 8% of the annual premium plus monthly fees of $3 to $5 for administrative costs. Finally, if you are forced to cash in a policy early, the insurer could penalize you with a stiff surrender charge amounting to as much as your entire investment in the first year or two.

Can I reduce these charges? Buy low-load policies directly from companies such as USAA Life (800-531-8000) and Ameritas Low-Load (800-255-9678). These policies' start-up costs consume only about 40% of first-year premiums. Even with low-load policies, you might pay $3 to $5 monthly and 2.5% to 3.5% of the premium to cover administrative expenses and the premium tax levied by every state. You can often cash in a low-load policy early at no charge.

Should I buy a policy from a company that promises to pay me dividends? With few exceptions, such dividends are paid by mutual insurance companies to owners of whole life policies. The dividends can be taken in cash or as additional paid-up insurance or used to reduce premiums. Nonparticipating policies, which are sold by stock companies, generally have lower-cost premiums. Mutual insurance companies won't guarantee payment of future dividends, but they do make projections based on their anticipation of investment performance and mortality experience.

How can I be sure that the insurer is healthy? Buy policies only from companies whose financial strength earns ratings of A+ or A in *Best's Insurance Reports*, available in most large libraries.

Why Disability Insurance Is Crucial

CONTRARY TO what life insurance agents may tell you, the coverage you need most isn't whole life, universal life, variable life or even universal-variable life. It's disability income insurance. This often overlooked coverage pays you a monthly income if you are unable to work because of injury or illness. Statistics show that disability is far more probable than death, especially if you are young or middle-aged. At age 42, for example, you are about four times more likely to be disabled for at least three months before retirement than you are to die. In fact, disability is sometimes called "living death," since your family's financial needs continue but you can't meet them unless you have insurance.

Unfortunately, there are plenty of temptations to put off obtaining coverage. It is expensive: the premium on an individual policy offering a $2,500-a-month benefit for a 40-year-old, nonsmoking male manager could run up to $2,000 a year. Also, you may mistakenly think you are fully protected by Social Security and possibly by your employer's group disability policy. But Social Security's disability criteria are so strict that only about 35% of those who apply for benefits actually qualify for them. And even if your employer offers insurance—as do 99% of large companies but less than 25% of businesses with fewer than 50 employees—there may still be holes in your coverage.

Some group policies don't cover you until you have worked for your employer for a year or two; others limit benefits to $2,000 a month. You can learn these details from the summary that federal law requires your employer's benefits administrator to make available. If your group plan seems skimpy, you can supplement it with an individual policy.

How much coverage do you need? In general, insurance experts recommend that disability insurance equal 60% to 70% of your before-tax earnings. Benefits should start 90 days after you become disabled (your savings presumably can carry you until then) and continue if necessary until you reach age 65. You probably cannot buy much more insurance than that anyway. To avoid attracting phony claims, most insurers will cover you only to the point at which your disability income from all sources, including Social Security and company benefits, would equal 70% of your current before-tax earnings. Still, that's better than it sounds. Benefits from a policy you buy with after-tax dollars are tax-free in contrast to income from a policy paid by your employer.

Equally important as the amount of coverage is the way your policy defines disability. Under the most generous definition, known as "own occ," insurers agree to pay full benefits if you can't work in your own occupation as long as you are under a physician's care. In contrast, a policy using the narrower "any occ" definition would pay only if you are unable to work in any occupation for which you are clearly suited. Under the any-occ rubric, for example, a practicing lawyer would not lose his benefits if he refused to work as, say, a taxi driver. But they would be cut off if he could teach law and declined, even if teaching would pay him an inadequate salary.

Insurers commonly compromise by splitting the definition and paying benefits under own-occ rules for the first one to five years of a disability and under any-occ rules thereafter. Not surprisingly, pure own-occ policies are 5% to 15% more expensive. The most expedient way to minimize the cost of your coverage is to prolong the so-called elimination period—the time you have to wait for benefits to begin after you become disabled. A 40-year-old nonsmoking manager could pay up to $1,500 a year in additional premiums for a 30-day waiting period rather than the more usual 90-day wait. Savings are less dramatic for longer waits. Stretching from 90 days to 180, for example, would typically cut the manager's premiums only about $100 a year.

Most financial advisers recommend that you choose a policy that stops paying benefits at age 65, because pension and Social Security retirement benefits kick in at that age. For premiums about 20% higher, you can select a benefit period that continues until you die. Such a policy would make sense if you are young and there is a possibility that a long-term disability would prevent you from building retirement benefits.

As with their other products, insurers tend to offer lots of options on disability policies. The most valuable (and often standard in a top-of-the-line policy) is a residual-benefits provision, which may add 20% to 25% to your premium. This option supplements your income if you are well enough to go back to work but not yet healthy enough to work at full capacity and earn full pay. Read your contract carefully. Some less generous policies pay so-called partial benefits—usually 50% of your full benefit—if you are partially disabled. Unlike residual benefits, which continue as long as needed, partial benefits typically terminate after three to six months.

Another valuable option is a cost-of-living adjustment (COLA), which will boost your premium 25% or so. With this rider, monthly benefits increase automatically to counter inflation, rising either at a specified rate or at the same rate as the consumer price index, up to a specified annual maximum. And you should insist on a policy that is at least guaranteed renewable, which means that the insurer cannot cancel your coverage as long as you pay your premiums or raise your premium unless it boosts premiums in general. A preferable alternative is a noncancelable policy, which guarantees that your policy cannot be revoked and that your premium cannot be increased at all.

CHAPTER FIVE

Taking Charge of Your Company Plans

LIKE MOST employees, you can rattle off your company's policy on vacations and sick days, perhaps even the medical expenses covered by its group health insurance. But also like most employees, you probably haven't a clue about the inner workings or potential benefits of the retirement package where you work. Don't blush, brush up. A thorough evaluation might reveal that your company's pension and tax-deferred savings plans are so chintzy you may as well start that long postponed job search—or at least begin building a separate nest egg of your own. You might also be surprised to discover that your retirement plans are much more generous than you had imagined. This chapter will help you size up your package, weigh your options and prepare for the taxing decisions and terminology that will attend the eventual payouts of your retirement. Suffice it to say that what you don't know now could cost you and your family dearly when you finally decide to call it quits.

For example, Wall Street's October 1987 crash rudely reaffirmed some tired truths about the stock market—and some fresh ones about the retirement packages of millions of employees. Chief among the lessons is that old-fashioned corporate paternalism is waning, and with it the cozy promise that if you put in your time, your company would look after your retirement. Today, the amount of money you take with you when you retire depends partly on how well you manage your interest in company savings plans—including profit-sharing and 401(k) accounts in which the employee, not the employer, bears the investment risk. Over the past decade or so, these thrift plans have grown three times as fast as traditional pensions whose benefits are guaranteed by employers, boom or bust.

The two types of retirement plans demand very different strategies. With your pension, your task is simply to understand how your benefits build and to use that knowledge to capitalize on a valuable asset. In your savings plans, the challenge is to balance investment risks with your desire to earn a high return on your contributions and those of your employer. The following should help make the decisions a little easier.

The Importance Of Your Pension

YOUR EMPLOYER typically calculates the size of your pension by multiplying a percentage of your final salary—say, 1%—by the number of years you were on the payroll. There is little you can do to manage your interest under this arrangement. Almost all employers fund their pensions entirely out of their own pockets, and all of them bear the responsibility both for investing the pension fund and for ensuring that the money to pay your retirement benefits is there when needed, regardless of the fund's investment performance. In the rare event that your company were to go bankrupt with an underfunded pension, a quasi-governmental insurance agency, the Pension Benefit Guaranty Corporation, would guarantee your benefits up to $2,437 a month.

A far more serious threat to many employees' future retirement income is their own readiness to change jobs. Since 1989, companies who offer pensions must begin to vest employees fully after their fifth year or gradually between their third and seventh year of service. When you leave a pension in mid-career, however, your benefits are frozen as of your departure. When you eventually start collecting checks from that pension, generally no earlier than age 55, inflation may have drastically eroded their value. So if you are within a decade of retirement, you should not change jobs or accept an early-retirement package without taking into account the value of the pension benefits you would forfeit.

How can you tell the value of what is essentially just a series of monthly checks beginning at some time in the future? The answer: your pension's current worth is the amount of money your employer would theoretically have to set aside today to pay you your promised monthly checks over your expected life span in retirement. Ask your employee-benefits department to tell you what your benefit would be if you retired now and what it would be if you retired at the time you had planned to leave.

For example, a 56-year-old executive currently earning $70,000, who had been with a typical company for 15 years, might be entitled to $1,300 a month. That benefit would require a pension reserve of $156,000. If the executive were to stay on the job until age 62 and received raises of 7% a year, he would retire on $3,310 a month. The fund would then need $343,000 when he reached age 62. That's the equivalent of $222,000 today, assuming the money was invested at 7.5%. An early-retirement package would have to offer him an additional $66,000 ($222,000 minus $156,000) just to compensate him for lost pension benefits.

The moral is that each year you continue working you earn far more in pension benefits than you might otherwise think. In a typical plan, the value of your pension would quadruple between ages 55 and 65. The primary reason: every year you work, your payout grows because it is based on an ever-larger percentage of a (presumably) ever-larger salary.

The Choices In Retirement Plans

THE NINE varieties of retirement plans listed here are all that most wage earners need to concern themselves with. With the exception of the defined-benefit pension, all of the plans require some caretaking—from occasional to intense.

PLAN TYPE	Major source of funding
Defined-benefit pension	Employer
Money-purchase pension	Employer; employee contributions sometimes allowed
Profit-sharing plan	Employer; employee contributions usually optional*
Savings plan	Employee*; company usually matches a portion of employee contributions
Employee stock-ownership plan (ESOP)	Employer
Tax-sheltered annuity (TSA or 403[b] plan)	Employee**; employer may contribute in some plans
IRA	Any salary or wage earner
Keogh plan	Self-employed people
Simplified employee pension (SEP)	Company; employee contributions may be optional ††

*Employee contributions are tax deductible if the plan is set up as a 401(k).

**Employee contributions are tax deductible.

†Those not covered by a company retirement or Keogh plan or who have adjusted gross income less than $25,000; ($40,000 for married couples).

†† Employee contributions are deductible in some SEPs.

Weighing An Offer Of Early Retirement

SUPPOSE YOUR boss asks you to consider taking early retirement in exchange for a package of tempting pension and fringe-benefit incentives. You probably will have only a month or two to accept or reject such an offer. So you will need to answer the following questions promptly and honestly. Am I ready to retire? If I turn down the package, will I be laid off anyway? Can I trust the company to live up to its promised fringe benefits?

Some employees have little alternative but to accept a package. Others may view an offer as the long-awaited inducement to clear their desks and leave a dead-end job. Either way, the paperwork can be staggering. Companies often send a targeted employee stacks of

Usual form of benefits	Where invested	Remarks
Annuity	Diversified among stocks, bonds, cash and sometimes real estate	Benefits depend on salary and length of service
Lump sum or installments	Same as defined-benefit pension	Benefits depend on size of contributions and investment performance of pension fund
Lump sum	Usually employee's choice of diversified stock fund, fixed-income account or company stock	Company contributions depend on size of company profits
Lump sum	Same as profit-sharing plan	Employees may be permitted to borrow a portion of vested benefits
Single payment of stock shares	Company stock	Starting at age 55, employees must be given a choice of other investments for a portion of their account balance
Employee's choice of lump sum or annuity	Usually employee's choice of mutual funds or insurance company annuities	Offered only by schools and nonprofit institutions
Lump sum or periodic withdrawals	Account with bank, brokerage, insurance company, mutual fund, credit union, savings and loan or trustee	Contributions are tax deductible for some IRA holders†
Same as IRA	Same as IRA	Contributions are tax deductible
Same as IRA	Same as IRA	Designed for small businesses

documents. Take them to your financial planner or accountant for help in assessing the package. Expect to pay $100 to $200 an hour for five to 30 hours of work, depending on the complexity of these key issues:

Pension. Consider as generous a package that pays you a pension equal to or greater than the one you would get by retiring as planned. The most fetching offers have such "sweetened pensions," in which the company calculates your benefit adding on three to five years to your age or tenure. Both types of sweeteners can increase your pension by as much as 30% over what you would have received by retiring early without a special arrangement.

Your company can't set back its early-retirement date for current employees or take away any vested benefits. But it can tinker with its pension formula. And firms with financial problems often do, curbing pensions for future staffers expecting to retire early. The most serious pension threat occurs if your employer sells out to another company with a less generous plan. Consider, as an example, a 53-year-old man who worked 28 years for a company that pays full early-retirement benefits to 30-year veterans age 55 or older. If his firm was acquired by another that pays unreduced pensions only to employees over 60, he might have to wait seven years, not two, for the same payout.

Health insurance. A 1986 law, known by its acronym of COBRA, requires that your employer at the very least continue your group health insurance coverage at your expense for up to 18 months after retirement, regardless of your age. Some firms keep paying the premiums when you retire early, but your dental coverage will almost certainly expire the day you quit. Employer-provided coverage is more comprehensive than a policy you could buy on your own—but also more expensive. Early-retirement deals that are the most appealing, but growing scarcer by the day, let you keep your employer's health insurance coverage for the rest of your life. If you are one of the fortunate few whose company will keep you covered, check whether the premiums, deductibles and benefits for an early retiree are the same as those for employees.

Retirees under 65 are especially vulnerable because their insurance isn't supplemented by Medicare, making it considerably more expensive for employers.

Parlaying Your Company Plans

UNLIKE PENSIONS, company savings and profit-sharing plans do not guarantee any particular retirement income. Instead, your employer establishes an investment account on your behalf and promises only to chip in a specified sum periodically. Otherwise, the responsibility for managing your account falls largely on you. You decide how to invest your account in the plan, and you take the consequences. If your investments tank, no kindly corporate patriarch stands by to make up the loss.

A consolation for shouldering the investment risk is that you can change jobs without gutting your payout. The sum that has built up in your account, usually tax-deferred, simply leaves with you. You can either roll it over into an IRA or into the corresponding plan offered by your new employer, if that plan permits. Whichever you choose, your money continues to grow free of taxes until withdrawal at retirement or upon disability.

The first decision you need to make in piloting a company plan is whether to get on board. Once you have money in the plan, it is quite difficult to get it out. In 401(k)s, for example, you can withdraw tax-deductible assets only in the case of financial hardship. And if you are younger than 59.5, you will owe the tax man a 10% penalty tax on top of his usual cut. Financial planners brush this demurral aside, however. One way or another, you have to save for your own retirement, they point out, and these savings plans give you more benefit for the buck than others. They allow your money to grow tax-free, which builds capital faster than similar investments outside the shelter of a company plan. In a 401(k), moreover, your contributions often are partially matched by your employer. In the most common formula, the employer kicks in 50 cents for each dollar you contribute—an instant 50% return.

Assuming that you do decide to participate in the plan, which investments should you choose? Generally, you must select among a family of funds, including some growth investments—such as a diversified stock fund or a fund invested entirely in the employer's stock—and one or two safer choices such as bond funds or guaranteed investment contracts (GICs), which are similar to bank CDs but backed by an insurance company. Rather than trying to adapt your retirement savings to whatever waves of fear or greed are sweeping the markets, you are better off adopting a conservative, diversified portfolio and sticking to it. Don't think of your company plan in isolation; ideally, investments in the plan should blend in with your outside holdings to create an overall portfolio that reflects your risk tolerance and goals.

If your outside holdings are large enough, it makes sense to keep most of your stocks there and to put safer, income-producing investments in your company plan. That way, you can soften the impact of setbacks in the stock market by writing off capital losses on your income tax return. You don't have that option if you suffer losses inside tax-sheltered retirement plans. Because of the limited investment choices that company plans offer, they may not blend smoothly with the rest of your portfolio. This is particularly true if—as is the case for many corporate employees—your company's plans make up the bulk of your retirement portfolio and absorb most of your annual retirement savings. In that event, you must construct a diversified portfolio that matches your goals as best you can with the choices available to you.

How To Make Your Payout Less Taxing

SO YOU served your time, built up your pension credits, religiously stashed a part of your check in the company savings plan and tended it wisely all these years. Now comes the gut-wrenching part: deciding how to take the money. At stake is probably the bulk of your retirement wealth. Since most choices open to you are irrevocable, if you choose wrong, you are stuck with the consequences for the rest of your life. For those reasons, you probably will want to have an experienced financial planner or accountant help you wrestle with the numbers and keep you from tripping over the tax laws. Together, you might consider the following series of questions:

Should you take your payout as a lump sum or an annuity? If your only company retirement plan is a pension, this decision has probably already been made for you. That's because most pensions pay benefits only in the form of a monthly annuity, which means equal monthly payments for the rest of your life. Only about one in five allows employees to take a lump sum instead. You are most likely to face the choice if your retirement package includes a savings plan such as profit sharing or a 401(k). Though such plans normally pay benefits as lump sums, your company may let you convert your account balance into an annuity. And even if your savings plan requires you to take a lump sum, you can always use the money to buy an annuity from an insurance company.

The annuity is guaranteed to last as long as you do. On the other hand, even with moderate inflation of 5% or so, fixed monthly payments will decline in purchasing power over the years. A 5% annual price rise will halve the real value of your checks after only 14 years. If you take a lump sum, however, you could put a portion in growth investments to preserve the purchasing power of your assets. Also, you may lean toward a lump sum if you want to leave money to your heirs.

In converting your benefits to a lump sum, a pension administrator calculates the amount it would take to pay you a monthly check for the rest of your expected life, as determined by actuarial tables, assuming the money earns a particular rate of return over time. But pension payments stop at the end of your life (or your surviving spouse's), not at the end of the actuarial life expectancy that is assigned to you at retirement. Thus an annuity is a bargain, comparatively speaking, if you manage to live longer than average, while a lump sum wins out if you die shortly after you retire. So if you are chronically ill, you should consider taking a lump sum; conversely, if you or your spouse are descended from a long line of nonagenarians, you might lean toward the annuity. If you're somewhere in between, read on.

Note that in calculating lump-sum conversions, employers use unisex life expectancy tables, which understate women's life expectancy. All else being equal, that makes an annuity a better deal for a woman than for a man. Interest rates can also determine whether a lump sum or an annuity is more advantageous. The higher the rate the plan's actuaries assume it can earn, the smaller the lump sum needed to pay a benefit. For example, in mid-1984, when interest rates were around 10.5%, a pension of $1,000 a month for a 60-year-old man translated to a lump sum of around $93,000. Recently, when interest rates were roughly 6%, the same benefit produced a lump sum of $128,000.

Many pension managers assume a conservative interest rate at the beginning of the year and stick with it. Thus in a year of rising interest rates, a lump sum offered by your plan late in the year could be disproportionately large. One simple way to tell would be to ask your life insurance agent how large an annuity benefit you could buy with the lump sum your pension is offering. To be competitive, insurers have to change their interest-rate assumptions frequently to match prevailing rates in the economy. So if interest rates are rising, you might be able to obtain a higher monthly payment from an insurer's annuity than from your pension, in spite of the insurer's sales charges and profit margin.

If you want an annuity, what kind should it be? The most common annuities are life only, which pays you a certain monthly amount until your death; joint and survivor, which assures that if you die first your spouse will continue to receive a certain amount until he or she dies; and life and period certain, which pays benefits for your lifetime or for a specified period—whichever is longer.

The option you choose will affect the size of your monthly checks. Life-only annuities pay the largest pensions but stop once you die; the other options continue to provide checks for your beneficiaries at the cost of reducing your income by 10% to 15% during your lifetime. One possible compromise: select the life-only option and buy a life insurance policy. Then when you die and the pension payments cease, the insurance benefits will provide for your spouse. (Under federal law, a married person cannot choose the life-only option without the written consent of his or her spouse. To make the insurance tactic work, get a notarized waiver of the joint-and-survivor option from your spouse.)

Take the example of a 63-year-old manager who must choose between a life-only pension of $30,000 or a $25,700 joint-and-survivor pension with his 63-year-old wife as beneficiary. Say that he selected the life-only option and bought a whole life policy that has an initial face value of about $130,000. (Level-premium whole life is required because term insurance is too expensive at older ages.) The couple could pocket an extra $50 a month in retirement income after the cost of the insurance. Upon his death, his wife would get the same income as under the joint-and-survivor pension option. To reduce the cost of this strategy, insist on a policy with minimum cash-value buildup and a face value that decreases over time. That way, as your beneficiary ages, he or she needs less life insurance proceeds to provide the same income because his or her life expectancy is growing shorter.

Which tax option should you take for a lump sum?
A lump-sum distribution need not be very large to push you into the top tax bracket. Luckily, the tax code lets you use one of two tax-saving tactics. First, if the lump sum makes up at least 50% of the value of your interest in a specific plan, such as a 401(k), you can roll the distribution over into an IRA within 60 days after receiving it. Your money will compound tax-free until you make withdrawals, which will be taxed as ordinary income. Thus, if you don't need to begin withdrawing money from the IRA for three to five years, the rollover is almost always preferable. Second, you can use a tax-saving device called forward averaging if you meet these conditions: your payout represents your entire interest in a plan; you have participated in the plan for at least five years; and you are 59.5.

If your lump sum makes it past all these checkpoints, it is taxed as if you had received it over five years instead of all at once. This is known as five-year forward averaging. If you were born before January 1, 1936, you can choose an even more capacious break, 10-year forward averaging. In both cases, you pay the total tax in the year you get the money but at a much lower rate than if the sum were taxed like the rest of your income. For example, with five-year forward averaging, a married couple with $30,000 of other income who received a lump sum of $150,000 would pay $30,398 in taxes instead of the $45,867 they would owe under ordinary tax tables. With 10-year averaging, you figure your taxes at 1986 rates, when brackets were as high as 50%. The couple in our example would pay a tax of $24,570 on their lump sum.

People over age 52 who participated in their employer's pension plan before 1974 have yet another option. They can elect to have the portion of the sum attributable to their pre-1974 contributions taxed as capital gains at the top 1986 rate of 20%. Your benefits department can tell you exactly how much qualifies as capital gains. Taxpayers in this category can then use five-year or 10-year forward averaging for the rest of their payout.

What methods give you the least tax? If none of your distribution qualifies as capital gains, the answer is 10-year averaging if your payout is less than $473,700. Above that amount the lower tax rates used in five-year averaging outweigh the greater bracket-lowering power of 10-year averaging. In other situations, the only way to choose between forward averaging and a rollover is to project the consequences of both into the future and see which rewards you with the most after-tax income.

The Art Of Withdrawing Gracefully

WHEN YOU start tapping your retirement savings, the accepted wisdom is to take out money in two waves. First draw on funds outside your IRA, company plan or any other tax-deferred investments, sheltering as much money in them as you can for as long as possible. Only later do you dip into these holdings. But tax law tampering by Congress, as with so many other facets of financial life, has complicated this simple approach.

The IRS issues guidelines for starting mandatory, taxable withdrawals at age 70.5 from all of your tax-deferred accounts—even if you're still working. Included are IRAs and company plans like pensions, profit-sharing accounts, 401(k)s and 403(b)s (for employees of tax-exempt organizations). An exception: most employees who turned 70.5 before January 1, 1988 may wait until they actually retire to start payouts from a company plan. The rules contain precise timetables for taking money out and revamped life expectancy tables for computing the amount. They also include a strong incentive to comply; underwithdrawals may be punished by a tax equal to 50% of the shortfall. As you approach the 70.5 mark, the following pointers can help you steer clear of the IRS and still manage your tax-favored accounts to your best advantage:

When. You must start withdrawals for the year you turn 70.5. If your 70th birthday falls after July 1, you must calculate a minimum withdrawal for the year. Generally, the deadline for taking your cash out is December 31. But you may postpone your first withdrawal until April 1 of the following year.

How much. The amount of the minimum withdrawal is based on both age and the total in each tax-deferred account at the beginning of the year for which you are making the withdrawal. Assume that you turned 70.5 and that your IRA was worth $100,000 on January 1. To determine the minimum withdrawal, you must divide this balance by the number given for your age in the life expectancy tables, found in IRS Publication No. 590, *Individual Retirement Arrangements.* Should you have a beneficiary, the appropriate table lists his or her age to arrive at a single number representing your joint life expectancy.

For your first withdrawal, you use age 71 for yourself and, let's say, 70 for your beneficiary. (The calculation is based on your ages at the end of the year for which the withdrawal is being made.) Thus your first mandatory withdrawal must be at least $4,950 ($100,000 divided by 20.2, the life expectancy for a 71-year-old IRA owner with a 70-year-old beneficiary). If you also have money in a company plan, your employer will compute the amount of the payout. It is your responsibility, however, to make sure that the IRS minimum is met. To avoid the penalty, ask your company's benefits supervisor for a statement that will ensure you of compliance.

Taking the optimum. The above calculations are the easy part. Like many retirees, you may be in the lowest 15% tax bracket. But two minimum payouts in a year—one in April and one at the end of December—may well push you into the 28% bracket. Thus, you may want to make your first withdrawal by December 31 instead of postponing it until April. A too large minimum payout could also backfire on your Social Security benefits. There's tax on up to 50% of your benefits if the total of your adjusted gross income, nontaxable interest, and half your Social Security exceeds $25,000 ($32,000 if you are married). If that total is over $34,000 ($44,000 for couples), you're taxed on up to 85% of benefits.

Massaging the tables. If continued tax-deferred growth is your objective, your choice of a beneficiary can result in a higher actuarial life expectancy and, consequently, lower annual payouts. If you have no beneficiary, for instance, your life expectancy at 71 would be 15.3 years, yielding an initial payout of $6,536 on a $100,000 account. But the joint life expectancy of a husband and wife, both 71, is 19.8 years; at 72 it is 18.9 years, with respective minimum payouts of $5,051 and $5,291. The IRS allows a maximum 10-year spread in age between you and your beneficiary, regardless of your actual age difference. This maneuver prevents you from drastically reducing your payouts by naming, say, a grandchild as your beneficiary. If the beneficiary is your spouse, however, real ages are always used.

Other wrinkles help you keep the minimum withdrawals down by stretching out your actuarial life expectancy. The tables use unisex figures and permit you to recalculate your life expectancy each year, extending your payouts (and tax shelter) over a longer period. It also helps ensure that you don't outlive your funds—based on the reassuring principle that the longer you live, the longer you are expected to go on living.

CHAPTER SIX

Managing Your Investments For a Lifetime

THERE WAS once a time when investing for retirement was a simple process of figuring out how much income you would need and then building a portfolio of high-quality bonds to deliver it. No longer. Bond coupons may give you reliable income, but they offer scant protection from inflation's erosion of your principal's purchasing power. Indeed, no single investment or technique can provide peace of mind and a topnotch return in today's volatile financial markets. Instead, a lifetime plan for prudently investing your wealth and conquering risk requires deft asset allocation—the proper mix of investments that not only preserve your capital but also make it grow over time.

Whether you are starting or unscrambling your retirement nest egg, the key decisions in the years ahead will hinge mainly on how old you are, where your financial assets are concentrated, your outlook for the economy and—most important—your tolerance for risk. The current moods of the stock and bond markets are but two of the factors you must weigh in deploying your money. You should also make gradual adjustments in your mix of assets to correspond with your changing needs for capital growth, steady income or a combination of the two as you draw nearer to the day when you finally call it a career.

Youth offers the greatest opportunities for you to start investing toward the goal of retirement because you can afford to be more daring than would be the case later in life. To enhance your returns and spread your risks, many advisers recommend that you set aside ample cash for emergencies and diversify the remainder of your funds among different types of growth-oriented investments. Heading the list are domestic and international stocks, real estate and mutual funds that specialize in these assets. If you believe in gold's efficacy as an inflation hedge, you might also consider adding a dollop of the heavy metal to your mix.

Between ages 45 and 50, you should begin moving to a middle-of-the-road strategy that stresses growth and income. Thus, you should keep about 50% of your money in stocks (or stock funds), which over time provide the highest inflation-adjusted return of any liquid asset. For additional income, you can put another 30% or so of your holdings into bonds and park the rest in cash equivalents such as a money-market fund. As you approach age 55 and become more concerned with capital preservation, you can reduce stocks to 30% of your portfolio and boost bonds to 40% and cash to 30%. Once you retire, conservative income-generating investments should dominate your portfolio: 50% in bonds and another 30% or so in money-market funds. To defend against outliving your capital, however, keep about 20% of your funds in stocks for growth.

Memories of Wall Street's 1987 crash haunt many investors who still shun stocks and the goal of capital appreciation, a key inflation hedge. Yet few recognize the varied ways in which they are vulnerable to other, less-shattering events such as a sudden rise in interest rates or an unexpected recession. Assessing your own exposure to such setbacks requires that you take a long hard look at what you own—and why.

Coming To Terms With Risk

NO MATTER what your age or how well you have diversified your portfolio, the challenge is to find your comfort zone—and to know that it will change as your temples gray and your career progresses. Astute asset allocation begins with a careful analysis of your investments and other aspects of your financial life to determine how each affects your exposure to the following risks:

Inflation risk. Rising prices will reduce the purchasing power of an investment. An annual inflation rate of 5% over 15 years will cut the value of $1,000 to $481. Overcautious investors who hoard assets in low-yielding investments such as savings accounts and money funds may not earn enough to outpace rising prices. Rising inflation also erodes the value of future income on investments with fixed payments, most notably long-term bonds.

Interest-rate risk. Rising interest rates will cause investments to drop in price. Higher rates make yields on existing bonds less attractive, so their market values decline. Rising rates also hurt stocks by making their dividend yields less appealing. People who invest borrowed money through margin accounts or who have other floating-rate debt increase their interest-rate risk because higher borrowing costs cut into their net profits.

Economic risk. Slower growth in the economy will cause investments to fall in price. Shares of emerging growth companies may shrink because they require a booming economy to sustain their robust earnings gains. Cyclical companies, such as automakers and chemical producers, cannot easily cut costs during a recession, so their shares may nosedive too. Economic downturns can also undercut junk bonds issued by financially weak firms that might default.

Market risk. This includes such factors as political developments and Wall Street fads that can batter investment markets. Tax law changes, trade agreements, program trading and the quirks of investor psychology all contribute to market risk, which has accounted for much of the stock market's day-to-day volatility. Gold also carries considerable market risk because its price moves sharply when political or military upheavals in other countries encourage the flight of capital.

Specific risk. This covers occurrences that may affect only a particular company or industry. For example, the death of a young company's founder could send the business into a tailspin. Individuals often take on a high degree of specific risk when they invest in a real estate partnership run by inexperienced general partners, or buy stock in a firm with a heavy debt burden. Specific risk also includes the chance that government regulation will harm a particular group of companies.

After uncovering the major risks in your portfolio, you can redeploy assets to reduce your exposure. Don't limit your financial inventory to investments that are kept in a brokerage account. Your earning power probably is by far your most valuable asset; equity in a home may come next. Many investors also have substantial assets invested in company pension plans or insurance policies with significant cash values. And entrepreneurs should take a close reading of the risks that threaten the value of their share of a small business.

Risk tends to creep up on even vigilant investors. Your holdings in a retirement plan or insurance policy may grow more quickly than you realize, particularly if you make regular contributions or reinvest your returns. But with this success comes a problem. Growth in one asset can throw a portfolio out of balance if other investments don't keep up. If a prolonged bull market boosts the value of your stockholdings, you may need to sell some shares to restore the balance between stocks and other assets. Similarly, when a single stock does extremely well, you had better bring yourself to shed some shares. Be especially wary of loading up on your company's stock through retirement and savings plans. If the company runs into trouble, both your job and your stock could be endangered at the same time. If you live in a one-company town, the value of your home may also be tied to the fortunes of that firm.

Keep a close eye on changes in your investment portfolio. A careful inspection may unearth important differences between investments that you thought were similar. For example, a study of mutual fund risk found that Fidelity Magellan and Twentieth Century Growth—two growth-stock funds with comparable investment objectives, returns and overall volatility—have responded quite differently when the economy has slowed. Magellan's holdings of large, well-established stocks have held up better than Twentieth Century's portfolio of smaller growth issues, which are especially sensitive to changes in the level of corporate profits.

To gauge your own situation, you will need to conduct a careful survey of your investments and other aspects of your finances. Here's a rundown of the strengths and weaknesses of various assets:

Stocks. They are vulnerable to the possibility that skittish investors will panic for some reason and drive share prices down en masse—an example of market risk. But risks related to inflation, interest rates or economic

QUESTIONS
• Are your assets diversified among fewer than four of these five major categories: stocks, real estate, gold, bonds and cash? If yes, score one point for each risk.
• Are more than 35% of your assets invested in any one of the five categories? If yes, score one point for each risk.
• Is at least 10% of your portfolio in assets such as gold, natural-resource stocks or high grade collectibles such as rare stamps? If no, score one point for inflation risk.
• Is at least 30% of your portfolio in investments such as growth stocks and real estate, which are likely to produce long-term capital gains that can outpace inflation? If no, score two points for inflation risk.
• Are your real estate and gold investments held primarily in assets such as gold-mining shares, REITs or real estate mutual funds, which fluctuate with the stock market? If yes, score one point for market risk.
• Do you generally keep at least 15% of your portfolio in cash equivalents such as Treasury bills or money-market funds? If no, score two points for interest rate risk.
• Is more than 30% of your portfolio composed of assets such as long-term bonds, certificates of deposit or annuities that provide fixed payments over a period of many years? If yes, score three points each for inflation and interest-rate risk.
• Do highly volatile zero-coupon bonds account for more than 30% of your fixed-income assets? If yes, score two points each for inflation and interest-rate risk.
• Do emerging growth stocks or junk bonds, which may fall sharply in a recession, account for more than 25% of your portfolio? If yes, score three points for economic risk.
• Do you switch money among different assets to try and catch the highs and lows of different investment markets? If yes, score two points for market risk.
• Do you use dollar-cost averaging or a similar plan that involves adding money to your investment portfolio at regular intervals? If no, score two points for market risk.
• Is more than 20% of your portfolio concentrated in a single industry? If yes, score three points each for economic risk, market risk, and specific risk.
• Do stocks or bonds issued by one company—including the one you work for—or shares in a single limited partnership account for more than 15% of your assets? If yes, score three points each for economic risk, market risk and specific risk.
• Does your share in a privately held business account for more than 30% of your portfolio? If yes, score one point for economic risk and four points for specific risk.
• Does a rental property account for more than 30% of your portfolio? If yes, score one point for economic risk and three points for specific risk.
• Do foreign stocks and shares of domestic companies with significant overseas sales account for less than 10% of your portfolio? If yes, score one point each for inflation and economic risk.
• Will you need access in the next three to five years to principal in volatile assets such as stocks or long-term bonds? If yes, score one point each for inflation, interest-rate, economic, and market risk.
• Do you have variable-rate loans such as mortgages or credit-card debt amounting to 30% or more of the value of your portfolio? If yes, score four points for interest-rate risk.
• Is 20% or more of your portfolio financed by loans or invested in highly leveraged assets such as options? If yes, score one point each for interest-rate and market risk.
TOTAL

Inflation Risk	Interest-Rate Risk	Economic Risk	Market Risk	Specific Risk

How Vulnerable Is [illegible] Retirement Portfolio?

MOST PEOPLE shield some of their investments against different types of risk, but few balance all of their assets so that they are well protected. This quiz can help you identify your points of vulnerability. With each question, you will accumulate points for one or more of the five major investment risks that are described in the main text. Write the points in the boxes at left. Then total the points for each risk and interpret your scores as follows: fewer than five points is low; five to 10 points, moderate; above 10 points, high. While you may want to vary your exposure to different risks, depending on your personal circumstances and outlook for the economy, any score above 10 points should set off alarm bells.

Once you have identified vulnerabilities, you can take steps to shore up your defenses. For example, say that you score high for inflation risk and low for market risk. You might balance your portfolio better by switching some cash from money funds to real estate, stocks or gold. While your risk of a temporary decline in the value of your portfolio will increase, you will have a better chance of outpacing inflation over the long term.

In answering the questions, don't forget about IRAs, 401(k) accounts, or any other savings or deferred-compensation plans. It may be difficult to pin down the value of some assets. For instance, you may have a universal life policy with an important investment component. Just make the best estimates that you can. It isn't necessary to be exact. But it is important that your inventory be as complete as possible.

growth may vary considerably from stock to stock. For example, a sharp increase in the inflation rate depresses stock prices because it may reduce the purchasing power of future dividends to shareholders. Also, inflation generally coincides with higher interest rates, which draw investors from stocks to bonds. Because firms such as retailers, consumer product manufacturers and service companies can pass cost increases along to customers relatively easily, they are more likely to prosper during periods of high inflation.

Slowing economic growth hurts some firms more than others. Manufacturing companies with high overhead, known as cyclicals, cannot easily cut costs when a recession slices sales, so their earnings quickly tail off. Many emerging growth companies also require an expanding economy to sustain their earnings growth and stock prices. By contrast, firms that sell necessities such as food or clothing often shine even in a lackluster economy, and their shares tend to hold up relatively well. Since foreign stocks are partly immune to changes in the American economy and markets, they may stand firm while U.S. stocks sink. But unlike domestic issues, shares denominated in foreign currencies carry the risk that a rising dollar will reduce their value.

Stocks also carry specific risks—those that are unique to a single firm or industry. Poor management or bad luck can dampen earnings or even bankrupt a company. And high-flying growth stocks are particularly vulnerable to earnings disappointments. One good way to reduce such risks is to buy shares that appear undervalued because they are selling at comparatively low price/earnings ratios or above-average yields.

Bonds. Their prices fall when interest rates rise. But the extent of the drop depends on a bond's maturity and the amount of its coupon. Short-term bonds fall slightly when interest rates move upward, and a high coupon also offers some protection against climbing rates. At the opposite extreme, zero-coupon bonds fall sharply when rates head higher. A recession generally brings lower interest rates, which boost bond prices. But some issues react negatively to the threat of an economic slowdown.

Junk bonds, in particular, may lose ground because investors fear that financially weak firms will default and fail to make payments of interest and principal to bondholders on time. U.S. Treasury and high-grade corporate bonds gain the most during hard times because income investors seek them out as safe havens.

Real estate investments. Although they tend to keep pace with inflation over time, they present other hazards. For example, if you own a rental property, you run the risk that you won't find a tenant. A real estate partnership that owns several properties in different regions can reduce such risks through diversification, but it may lose value if tax changes or a recession drive down property values across the country. And real estate investment trusts and real estate mutual funds fluctuate with the stock market as well as with property values.

Gold and other hard assets. The price of gold can skyrocket when inflation rises rapidly. Between 1968 and 1988, the consumer price index posted nine annual spurts of 6% or more. During those years, gold rewarded investors with an average gain of 34%. Gold-mining stocks are more volatile than the metal itself and expose investors to other risks. A South African miners' strike, for example, might boost the price of bullion but cut profits at some mining companies. Other tangibles present their own problems. While antiques or rare stamps may outpace inflation in the long run, prices of specialized items such as baseball cards are largely subject to collectors' whims.

Five Investing Mistakes To Avoid

ONCE YOU have identified the risks in your portfolio, you can adjust them to suit your particular investment goals and temperament. That might mean reducing your interest-rate risk by lightening up your large holdings of long-term bonds. Then again, you may decide to shoulder new risks in pursuit of higher profits over time. Even seasoned investors frequently make mistakes. But common errors you should try to avoid include the following:

Having too much money in your company's stock. Investors who concentrate a sizable share of their assets in any single stock are courting trouble. Many make the mistake—often without even knowing it—because they invest heavily in the shares of the corporation they work for through vehicles such as 401(k), profit-sharing and other tax-deferred plans.

Leaving too much money in cash. Some investors escape the perils of stock market volatility, bond defaults and real estate slumps by keeping the bulk of their assets in cash. But they often overlook an even more relentless threat—inflation. Cash equivalents such as Treasury bills and money-market accounts offer no chance for capital gains that can outpace rising prices.

Assembling a portfolio piecemeal. You may be a genius at spotting enticingly undervalued stocks or choosing top-performing mutual funds. But a collection of great individual investments does not always provide the balance your portfolio needs. If you have already loaded up on stocks, for example, you probably should pass up a promising new stock issue and buy income-generating bonds or real estate instead.

Buying more investments than you can monitor. To diversify fully, you may be tempted to own so many issues that you do not have time to follow them all carefully. Or you may buy investments for which accurate information is hard to obtain. Remember that less can be more. Choose a mutual fund or two instead of a host of individual stocks to fill out the gaps in your diversification plan.

Overlooking important assets. Many investors focus their diversification efforts too narrowly, excluding major assets such as their rising earning power, their appreciating home and their mounting tax-deferred accounts. But such assets may be the most valuable. If your IRA is stashed in long-term bonds and cash, for example, you should consider tilting your remaining assets toward growth-oriented investments.

CHAPTER SEVEN

Keeping It All in the Family

IT'S STRANGE but true: about seven of 10 adults have life insurance, but only a third have wills. The most plausible explanation for such faulty forward planning is that insurance is sold and wills are not. Since lawyers don't hawk their wares door to door, you will just have to motivate yourself to provide a secure financial future for your family. Consider the possible consequences if you decide to do nothing:

Thy will won't be done. Should you die without a will, your heirs' inheritances will be determined under state laws of intestacy, which may not match your own notion of who should get what. In most states, your assets are apportioned among your spouse and children, often with half to two-thirds going to your kids.

The tax man grabbeth. Even if you write a will, your estate may not escape taxation. By using trusts, however, a married couple can pass as much as $1.2 million to their heirs free of federal estate tax, with its grim-reaper rates running as high as 55%.

Suffer ye children. A solid estate plan will protect and preserve property you leave to children or disabled heirs. You can also spare your heirs the inconvenience of probate, the legal process in which your will is proved valid and your assets are inventoried in court.

To accomplish all of this, you will need the help of an attorney who's an expert on estate planning. Finding one may be difficult. Ask your friends, relatives, accountant or financial planner for recommendations, or call your city's bar association and ask for the telephone number of the local estate planning council. You will be able to communicate more effectively with your lawyer if you understand the fundamentals discussed below.

Preparing A Simple Will

MANY PEOPLE never get around to writing a will for fear of confronting their own mortality. Others figure they don't need one if they own all of their assets jointly. But their survivors eventually learn that joint ownership is no substitute for a well-drafted will. And the peace of mind that it provides comes at a modest price. Simple wills for a husband or wife cost around $150 each. A more elaborate will might cost up to $400, depending on the complexity of your finances.

Assume, for example, that an elderly widow puts her son's name on her bank account, making him joint owner of the balance, for the express purpose of allowing him to deposit checks for her. She may tell him to divide the money equally with his siblings after she's gone, but what if he decides to keep the cash? His brothers and sisters can take him to court, but litigation is costly and time consuming and may not be worthwhile unless a large amount of money is at stake.

Married couples shouldn't rely solely on joint ownership either. If a childless couple were involved in an accident in which the husband was killed while the wife survived for another day, the husband's half of the couple's joint property would automatically pass to his wife. But unless she managed somehow to scribble a will as she lay on her deathbed, all of the couple's assets would go to the wife's relatives after her death, leaving his family with nothing. Couples with minor children also need wills, despite the fact that their jointly held property will go to their children under state laws of intestacy if they die together. It's in a will that you nominate guardians to care for your children and manage their inheritances. If you don't name caretakers for your kids, the probate judge will appoint guardians of his or her own choosing for the children and their assets.

You also nominate the executor of your estate in your will. It is his or her responsibility to pay your debts, file tax returns and disburse assets to your heirs after you are gone. If you already have a will, examine it periodically to make sure it still reflects your wishes.

When To Review Your Will

THE SOUR old Scrooge who revises his will weekly to avenge every slight may have a point. Most people seldom bother to review their wills at all, passing up the chance to make necessary changes. You and your lawyer should review your will every three years or so, but examine it sooner if you've grown much richer or suffered a serious financial setback.

You should also review your will after the birth of a child or the death of a spouse or other beneficiary. An examination is also in order after tax law changes. And bear in mind that your will may be partially invalidated if you marry or divorce after writing it. If you move to another state, ask a local lawyer to make certain your will complies with your new home state's statutes. He or she can also tell you if you've done all you can to diminish state death taxes.

You needn't tear up your old will and begin anew to make minor changes. For example, you can add or remove a beneficiary, change the amount of someone's bequest or replace an executor or guardian by asking your attorney to draft an amendment to your will called a codicil. Like wills, codicils must be signed and witnessed. After you've added a couple of codicils, draw up a fresh will to avoid possible confusion. Whatever you do, don't alter the original copy of your will yourself. If you do, its validity can come into question.

Moreover, you shouldn't stash the original in your safe-deposit box; banks in many states will seal boxes until a court orders them opened. If you include burial instructions in your will, your survivors may not get to read them before your funeral. Leave the original copy of your will with your lawyer, who may store it in his office or, better yet, with other wills in a bank vault. Or you can file your will at your county probate court for a small fee. If you wish, you can give your executor a copy of your will. To make reviewing it easy, keep copies in your safe-deposit box as well as at home.

Trusts That Care For Heirs

IF YOUR heirs are very young, disabled or simply disinclined to manage money, you will shortchange them if you do nothing more than write a rudimentary will. Say that you and your spouse die and leave your assets to your minor children. The guardian of their property named in your will must report expenditures and investments on the children's behalf to a judge. This may prevent the guardian from stealing or dissipating the children's inheritances. But it also gives a judge who is unfamiliar with your financial goals and investment philosophy power over how your legacy is managed and spent.

That's one reason why it's advisable to create a trust in your will to hold your children's inheritances. If you do, you needn't name a guardian of your children's assets because a trustee you select will follow instructions that you set down in your trust document. Another advantage of creating a trust is that you can keep the trust principal out of your children's hands until you think they will be mature enough to manage money. If you leave property to your children in your will, on the other hand, they can claim their inheritances when they reach the age of majority, which is 18 in most states.

Many people shy away from trusts because they associate them with the superrich. In reality, a married couple might pay as little as $250 to establish trusts for their children. Trusts are quite flexible, and a lawyer can draft yours to fit your family's particular needs. Before you read about types of trusts, it may be helpful to understand just how trusts work.

A trust is a legal device that holds property placed in it by a person called the grantor for the benefit of one or more beneficiaries. The grantor sets forth instructions for the management of the trust and the disbursement of its income and principal in a document, called the trust agreement, drawn up by an attorney. The grantor also chooses a trustee to carry out his wishes.

There are two basic types of trusts, testamentary and living (sometimes called *inter vivos*). A *testamentary trust* is created in your will and takes effect upon your death. A *living trust* operates during your lifetime. Living trusts may be either revocable or irrevocable. With a *revocable trust,* you continue to control the trust property, meaning you can change the trust's provisions, terminate it or, in some cases, even serve as trustee. Once you establish an *irrevocable trust,* however, you cannot control assets in it or tinker with its provisions.

As a result, property in an irrevocable trust isn't included in your estate for the purpose of calculating estate taxes. (You may incur gift tax when you put property into an irrevocable trust.) Assets in a revocable trust are part of your taxable estate. A testamentary trust for your minor children that becomes irrevocable upon your death is included in your taxable estate because you controlled the property during your lifetime.

A trust is only as effective as the trustee you choose. The ideal trustee is financially savvy and has your children's best interests at heart. Your relatives and friends will probably agree to serve without any compensation. Institutional trustees such as banks and trust companies will generally levy annual fees of about 1% of a trust's assets up to $1 million. After that, the larger the trust, the smaller the trustee's percentage.

Sidestepping Estate Taxes

IF YOU fail to draw up an airtight estate plan, the IRS may claim a more than generous share of your estate. The top rate is currently 55% on taxable estates of more than $3 million. In addition, state death taxes range from zero to 30%. Still, with proper planning, most estates can escape federal and state taxation. Your $600,000 exclusion from federal taxes includes the sum of taxable gifts you make while you are alive as well as the estate you leave when you die. You can make tax-free gifts up to $10,000 a year each to as many people as you like; married couples giving jointly may bestow as much as $20,000. You can also make unlimited tax-free gifts to charity and payments to health-care and educational institutions to cover a relative's or friend's bills.

In addition, you may make gifts of any size and leave an estate of any value to your spouse tax-free. If your spouse is not adept at money management, you might want to leave assets to him or her in a trust that qualifies for the marital deduction, meaning that its contents aren't subject to estate tax. There are two basic types of marital deduction trusts. With a *general power of appointment trust,* your spouse decides which heirs get the trust's assets after he or she dies. With a *QTIP trust* (for qualified terminable interest property), you choose your spouse's eventual heirs.

If you leave everything to your spouse, however, you may succeed only in postponing estate taxes until his or her death. As a result, more complicated tax planning may be necessary. You can eliminate or at least reduce estate taxes by removing assets from your estate. This is accomplished by making tax-free gifts during your lifetime, including charitable contributions in your will and placing property in trusts.

A married couple can pass as much as $1.2 million to their heirs tax-free if both spouses fully utilize their $600,000 exemptions. Take, for example, a couple with *revocable bypass trusts* (sometimes called family or credit-shelter trusts). If the husband dies or becomes unable to manage his financial affairs, assets he owns of up to $600,000 go into his trust. His wife will receive income from the trust and is entitled, say, to as much as 5% or $5,000 of the principal, whichever is greater, each year. In addition, the trustee has the discretion to give her the principal that she needs to support herself or pay medical bills. After her death, the couple's children become the trust's beneficiaries. No estate tax will be due because the trust isn't included in the wife's estate and the amount contributed to it by her husband was within his $600,000 exemption. If the wife dies or becomes incapacitated first, her trust is funded in a similar way for her husband's benefit.

You can also trim your tax liability by placing property in an irrevocable living trust. The hitch: few people can afford to relinquish control of real estate, securities or other assets years before their death. Many people, however, can afford to transfer the ownership of their life insurance policies to an *irrevocable life insurance trust.* Upon your death, your life insurance proceeds go into such a trust untaxed. Your spouse typically receives income from the trust for life and can tap its principal if necessary. After he or she dies, the assets go to heirs named in your trust agreement.

There's one catch, however. If you die within three years of establishing an irrevocable life insurance trust, the insurance proceeds are included in your taxable estate. For that reason, attorneys often include a clause in the trust agreement stating that should you die within three years, the insurance will go directly to your spouse or into a trust for his or her benefit. The trust is included in his or her estate.

You can also remove assets from your taxable estate by making gifts to charity during your lifetime or in your will. If you give during your lifetime, you can be a philanthropist at wholesale prices because you get an income tax deduction and remove the property from your estate. You can also experience the joy of giving, which you cannot do if you leave money to a charity in your will. You can even give assets to a charity and keep on getting income from them by establishing a trust or buying an annuity from the charity. Of course, because you retain income from your gift, the tax deductions you receive will be smaller than what you might have gotten with an outright gift.

If you establish a *charitable remainder unitrust*, you receive an amount determined annually by multiplying a fixed percentage that you select when you create the trust by the market value of the trust's assets. After your death, payments end or a beneficiary can continue to receive the income from the trust. When he or she dies, the trust's property passes to the charity. In general, charities welcome only sizable remainder unitrusts that are worth $25,000 or more.

Charitable remainder annuity trusts work much like unitrusts but pay out a fixed amount each year. Appreciated property producing little or no income makes the best gift. If you sold it and reinvested the proceeds for higher income, you would incur a taxable capital gain. But if a charitable trust sells the property, no tax is due. For smaller donors, some charities offer pooled income funds that operate much like mutual funds. Many accept initial donations as small as $5,000.

Altruists whose hearts are bigger than their bank accounts should also consider charitable gift annuities. Many tax-exempt organizations issue these contracts for contributions as small as $1,000. In exchange for your donation, the charity pays you a fixed amount each year for life. The younger you are when you buy the annuity, the lower your return. For example, a 50-year-old would receive 6.5% for life while a 90-year-old would collect 14%. You would receive more income if you bought an annuity from an insurance company, but you would not get any income tax deductions or an estate tax break.